Sigmund Freud was born in 1856 in Moravia; between the ages of four and eighty-two his home was in Vienna: in 1938 Hitler's invasion of Austria forced him to seek asylum in London, where he died in the following year. His career began with several years of brilliant work on the anatomy and physiology of the nervous system. He was almost thirty when, after a period of study under Charcot in Paris, his interests first turned to psychology, and another ten years of clinical work in Vienna (at first in collaboration with Breuer, an older colleague) saw the birth of his creation, psycho-analysis. This began simply as a method of treating neurotic patients by investigating their minds, but it quickly grew into an accumulation of knowledge about the workings of the mind in general, whether sick or healthy. Freud was thus able to demonstrate the normal development of the sexual instinct in childhood and, largely on the basis of an examination of dreams, arrived at his fundamental discovery of the unconscious forces that influence our everyday thoughts and actions. Freud's life was uneventful, but his ideas have shaped not only many specialist disciplines, but the whole intellectual climate of the last half-century.

SIGMUND FREUD

TWO SHORT ACCOUNTS OF PSYCHO-ANALYSIS

(FIVE LECTURES ON PSYCHO-ANALYSIS AND
THE QUESTION OF LAY ANALYSIS)

Translated and Edited by
JAMES STRACHEY

PENGUIN BOOKS

Penguin Books Ltd, Harmondsworth, Middlesex, England
Viking Penguin Inc., 40 West 23rd Street, New York, New York 10010, U.S.A.
Penguin Books Australia Ltd, Ringwood, Victoria, Australia
Penguin Books Canada Limited, 2801 John Street, Markham, Ontario, Canada L3R 1B4
Penguin Books (N.Z.) Ltd, 182–190 Wairau Road, Auckland 10, New Zealand

—

Uber Psychoanalyse first published Vienna 1910
First English translation (by H. W. Chase) published under the title *The Origin and
Development of Psychoanalysis* in the *American Journal of Psychology* 1910
Separate offprint. Worcester, Mass. 1910
Present English translation (by James Strachey) published under the title *Five Lectures
on Psychoanalysis* in Standard Edition of Freud's Works by the Hogarth Press and the
Institute of Psycho-Analysis, London, 1957

—

Die Frage der Laienanalyse first published Vienna 1926
First English translation (by A. P. Maerker-Branden) published under the title
The Problem of Lay-Analyses, New York 1927
New English translation (by N. Procter-Gregg) published under the title *The Question
of Lay Analysis*, London 1947; New York 1950
Present English translation (by James Strachey) published under the title *The Question
of Lay Analysis*, in Standard Edition of Freud's Works by the Hogarth Press and the
Institute of Psycho-Analysis, London, 1959

—

Two Short Accounts of Psycho-Analysis published
in Pelican Books 1962
Reprinted 1963, 1966, 1968, 1970, 1972, 1974, 1976, 1977, 1981, 1983, 1984, 1986

—

Translation of *Five Lectures on Psycho-Analysis* copyright © A. S. Strachey, 1957
Translation of *The Question of Lay Analysis* copyright © A. S. Strachey, 1959
Preface, Biographical Note, and Chronological Table copyright © A. S. Strachey, 1962
Two Short Accounts of Psycho-Analysis copyright © Sigmund Freud Copyrights, 1962
All rights reserved

—

Printed and bound in Great Britain by
Cox & Wyman Ltd, Reading
Set in Linotype Pilgrim

CONTENTS

PREFACE

ALL through his life Freud was willing and ready to publish general accounts of his discoveries and views which should be non-technical and understandable by people of ordinary knowledge and intelligence. More than a dozen of these semi-popular accounts could be named, among them the very last of his writings. The present volume contains two of these works, which are separated in time by a gap of nearly twenty years and which for that reason give us an opportunity of observing the development of psycho-analysis from a relatively early date to a relatively late one.

The most important of all these expository works was the long series of lectures which Freud delivered in Vienna University during the First World War and which were published in England under the title of *Introductory Lectures on Psycho-Analysis*. The first of the two works before us here is another series of lectures, much shorter and delivered some years earlier, in 1909. At that time Freud was very little known outside narrow circles in Vienna and Zürich, and it came as an agreeable surprise to him when, in December 1908, he received an invitation to deliver a series of five lectures in America. The invitation came from Stanley Hall, President of Clark University at Worcester, Massachusetts, who was known as an academic and experimental psychologist, and the occasion was to be the University's celebration, in September 1909, of the twentieth year of its foundation. Freud describes how 'as I stepped on to the platform at Worcester . . . it seemed like the realization of some incredible day-dream: psycho-analysis was no longer a product of delusion, it had become a valuable part or reality'. Jung, who was at that time Freud's leading lieutenant, went with him to Worcester, delivered two lectures there, and, like

Freud, received an honorary degree. Others of Freud's supporters who were later to become well known were also there – Ernest Jones, A.A. Brill, and Sándor Ferenczi. To the last of these Freud elsewhere attributes some responsibility for the lectures: 'In the morning, before the time had come for my lecture to begin, we would walk together in front of the University building and I would ask him to suggest what I should talk about that day. He thereupon gave me a sketch of what, half an hour later, I improvised in my lecture.' In fact the lectures, which were delivered in German, were not written down by Freud till the end of the year, after his return to Vienna; but Ernest Jones tells us that the written version did not differ much from the oral one. Their first publication was in English (translated by H. W. Chase) in the *American Journal of Psychology* in 1910, and the German original appeared shortly afterwards. In the course of the following years the lectures had an extensive circulation and were translated into many languages, and this was Freud's first emergence into the field of international science. The climate of opinion into which he was breaking may be judged by the contemporary comment of a leading official of a Canadian university: 'An ordinary reader would gather that Freud advocates free love, removal of all restraints, and a relapse into savagery.' An ordinary reader today is unlikely to find the lectures so shocking; though he may well learn much from them. Indeed, while many additions – complications and refinements – were to be made to psychoanalysis in the years that lay ahead, the *Five Lectures* present an excellent preliminary outline of the subject, which calls for little correction.

The second of our present two works, *The Question of Lay Analysis*, was born into a much-changed climate of opinion. Freud had become a celebrity, except, perhaps, in Vienna: psycho-analysis was studied everywhere, its practitioners were organized in all the principal countries in the world. Actually, however, the work we are considering was precipitated by an event which can only be described as parochial. In the late spring of 1926 proceedings were begun in Vienna against Theodor Reik, a prominent non-medical member of the Vienna Psycho-Analytical Society, for whom Freud had a special regard. He was charged, on information laid by someone whom he had been treating analytically, with a breach of an old Austrian law against 'quackery' – a law which made it illegal for a person without a medical degree to treat patients. Freud at once intervened energetically on behalf of Reik. He argued the position privately with an official of high standing and went on to compose the present work, which was published the same autumn. Partly because the evidence was unsatisfactory, but partly too, perhaps, as a result of Freud's intervention, the proceedings were dropped.

Thus the practical importance of this issue is restricted to those countries in which therapeutic activity is legally restricted to qualified doctors. Such is not the case, for instance, in England, where anyone may practise any form of therapy, provided he does not profess to be a doctor and is prepared to meet the normal legal responsibilities involved in his proceedings. But this issue gave rise to a still more restricted controversy – within the psycho-analytic world itself. Some analysts disagreed with Freud's thesis and held that only qualified doctors should practise therapeutic analysis. This was particularly so in America where, though in some States there is no anti-quackery law, the American Psycho-analytic Association does not admit non-doctors to its 'active membership'. Such, once more, is not the case in England, for the British Psycho-Analytical Society allows the admission of members without a medical qualification provided they undertake always to work under a doctor's supervision.

But these local and domestic arguments are in any case of no particular interest to the general reader, nor are they the reason for presenting him with this example of Freud's work.

It happens, however, that Freud made use of this occasion for giving the very best of his shorter general expositions of psycho-analysis. It is not only clear and comprehensive but entertaining, and its dialogue form affords plenty of scope for the lively irony of Freud's writing. It has, too, the advantage of giving an account of Freud's views in the latest stage of their development.

A comparison between these two works should therefore prove instructive. The *Five Lectures* will be found to contain a sketch of Freud's fundamental hypotheses of the dynamic nature of mental processes and of their being subject to the law of causality, and a view of the observations which led him to the distinction between conscious and unconscious events in the mind and to the concepts of conflict and repression. They also give some account of the method Freud devised for investigating the contents of the unconscious and of the findings which resulted – in particular, infantile sexuality and the Oedipus complex. All of these topics are dealt with again, but much more extensively, and with a surer hand, in the *Lay Analysis*. Here, too, the question of the aetiology of the neuroses comes up for more detailed discussion, as well as such peculiarly abtruse clinical problems as those of anxiety and the sense of guilt and, on the theoretical side, the nature of instinct and the operation of the pleasure and reality principles. The main underlying difference between the two expositions is, however, that in the later one Freud adopts what he had only recently devised – his *structural* description of the mind, with its functional division into an id, an ego, and a super-ego. This new method of formulating things will be found greatly to clarify both the theoretical and clinical sides of the subject. Finally, in view of the topic of its central argument, Freud here gives a far more detailed account than in the earlier work of the nature of the therapeutic process in analysis and of its mechanism.

SIGMUND FREUD
A SKETCH OF HIS LIFE AND IDEAS

SIGMUND FREUD was born on 6 May 1856 in Freiberg, a small town in Moravia, which was at that time a part of Austria-Hungary. In an external sense the eighty-three years of his life were on the whole uneventful and call for no lengthy history.

He came of a middle-class Jewish family and was the eldest child of his father's second wife. His position in the family was a little unusual, for there were already two grown-up sons by his father's first wife. These were more than twenty years older than he was and one of them was already married, with a little boy; so that Freud was in fact born an uncle. This nephew played at least as important a part in his very earliest years as his own younger brothers and sisters, of whom seven were born after him.

His father was a wool-merchant and soon after Freud's birth found himself in increasing commercial difficulties. He therefore decided, when Freud was just three years old, to leave Freiberg, and a year later the whole family settled in Vienna, with the exception of the two elder half-brothers and their children, who established themselves instead in Manchester. At more than one stage in his life Freud played with the idea of joining them in England, but nothing was to come of this for nearly eighty years.

In Vienna during the whole of Freud's childhood the family lived in the most straitened conditions; but it is much to his father's credit that he gave invariable priority to the charge of Freud's education, for the boy was obviously intelligent and was a hard worker as well. The result was that he won a place in the 'Gymnasium' at the early age of nine, and for the last six of the eight years he spent at the school he was regularly top of his class. When at the age of seventeen he passed out of school his career was still undecided; his education so far had been of the most general kind, and, though he seemed in any case destined for the University, several faculties lay open to him.

Freud insisted more than once that at no time in his life did he feel 'any particular predilection for the career of a doctor. I was moved, rather', he says, 'by a sort of curiosity, which was, however, directed more towards human concerns than towards natural objects.' Elsewhere he writes: 'I have no knowledge of having had any craving in my early childhood to help suffering humanity. ... In my youth I felt an overpowering need to understand something of the riddles of the world in which we live and perhaps even to contribute something to their solution.' And in yet another passage in which he was discussing the sociological studies of his last years: 'My interest, after making a lifelong *détour* through the natural sciences, medicine, and psychotherapy, returned to the cultural problems which had fascinated me long before, when I was a youth scarcely old enough for thinking.'

What immediately determined Freud's choice of a scientific career was, so he tells us, being present just when he was leaving school at a public reading of an extremely flowery essay on 'Nature', attributed (wrongly, it seems) to Goethe. But if it was to be science, practical considerations narrowed the choice to medicine. And it was as a medical student that Freud enrolled himself at the University in the autumn of 1873 at the age of seventeen. Even so, however, he was in no hurry to obtain a medical degree. For his first year or two he attended lectures on a variety of subjects, but gradually concentrated first on biology and then on physiology. His very first piece of research was in his third year at the University, when he was deputed by the Professor of Comparative Anatomy to investigate a detail in the anatomy of the eel, which involved the dissection of some four hundred specimens. Soon afterwards he entered the Physiological Laboratory under Brücke, and worked there happily for six years. It was no doubt from him that he acquired the main outlines of his attitude to physical science in general. During these years Freud worked chiefly on the anatomy of the central nervous system and was already beginning to produce publications. But it was becoming obvious that no livelihood which would be sufficient to meet the needs of the large family at home was to be picked up from these laboratory studies. So at last, in 1881, he decided to take his medical degree, and a year later, most unwillingly, gave up his position under Brücke and began work in the Vienna General Hospital.

What finally determined this change in his life was something more urgent than family considerations: in June 1882 he became engaged to be married, and thenceforward all his efforts were directed towards making marriage possible. His fiancee, Martha Bernays, came of a well-known Jewish family in Hamburg, and though for the moment she was living in Vienna she was very soon obliged to return to her remote North-German home. During the four years that followed, it was only for brief visits that he could have glimpses of her, and the two lovers had to content themselves with an almost daily interchange of letters. Freud now set himself to establishing a position and a reputation in the medical world. He worked in various departments of the hospital, but soon came to concentrate on neuroanatomy and neuropathology. During this period, too, he published the first inquiry into the possible medical uses of cocaine; and it was this that suggested to Koller the drug's employment as a local anaesthetic. He soon formed two immediate plans: one of these was to obtain an appointment as *Privatdozent*, a post not unlike that of a university lecturer in England, the other was to gain a travelling bursary which would enable him to spend some time in Paris where the reigning figure was the great Charcot. Both of these aims, if they were realized, would, he felt, bring him real advantages, and in 1885, after a hard struggle, he achieved them both.

The months which Freud spent under Charcot at the Salpêtrière (the famous Paris hospital for nervous diseases) brought another change in the course of his life and this time a revolutionary one. So far his work had been concerned entirely with physical science and he was still carrying out histological studies on the brain while he was in Paris. Charcot's interests were at that period concentrated mainly on hysteria and hypnotism. In the world from which Freud came these subjects were regarded as barely respectable, but he became absorbed in them, and, though Charcot himself looked at them purely as branches of neuropathology, for Freud they meant the first beginnings of the investigation of the mind.

On his return to Vienna in the spring of 1886 Freud set up in private practice as a consultant in nervous diseases, and his long-delayed marriage followed soon afterwards. He did not, however, at once abandon all his neuropathological work: for several more years he studied in particular the cerebral palsies of children, on which he became a leading authority. At this period, too, he produced an important monograph on aphasia. But he was becoming more and more engaged in the treatment of the neuroses. After experimenting in vain with electro-therapy, he turned to hypnotic suggestion, and in 1888 visited Nancy to learn the technique used with such apparent success there by Liébeault and Bernheim. This still proved unsatisfactory and he was driven to yet another line of approach. He knew that a friend of his, Dr Josef Breuer, a Vienna consultant considerably his senior, had some ten years earlier cured a girl suffering from hysteria by a quite new procedure. He now persuaded Breuer to take up the method once more, and he himself applied it to several fresh cases with promising results. The method was based on the assumption that hysteria was the product of a psychical trauma which had been forgotten by the patient; and the treatment consisted in inducing her in a hypnotic state to recall the forgotten trauma to the accompaniment of appropriate emotions. Before very long Freud began to make changes both in the procedure and in the underlying theory; this led eventually to a breach with Breuer, and to the ultimate development by Freud of the whole system of ideas to which he soon gave the name of psycho-analysis.

From this moment onwards – from 1895, perhaps – to the very end of his life, the whole of Freud's intellectual existence revolved around this development, its far-reaching implications, and its theoretical and practical repercussions. It would, of course, be impossible to give in a few sentences any consecutive account of Freud's discoveries and ideas, but an attempt will be made presently to indicate in a disconnected fashion some of the main changes he has brought about in our habits of thought. Meanwhile we may continue to follow the course of his external life.

His domestic existence in Vienna was essentially devoid of episode: his home and his consulting rooms were in the same house from 1891 till his departure for London forty-seven years later. His happy marriage and his growing family – three sons and three daughters – provided a solid counterweight to the difficulties which, to begin with at least, surrounded his professional career. It was not only the nature of his discoveries that created prejudice against him in medical circles; just as great, perhaps, was the effect of the intense anti-semitic feeling which dominated the official world of Vienna: his appointment to a university professorship was constantly held back by political influence.

One particular feature of these early years calls for mention on account of its consequences. This was Freud's friendship with Wilhelm Fliess, a brilliant but unbalanced Berlin physician, who specialized in the ear and throat, but whose wider interests extended over human biology and the effects of periodic phenomena in vital processes. For fifteen years, from 1887 to 1902, Freud corresponded with him regularly, reported the development of his ideas, forwarded him long drafts outlining his future writings, and, most important of all, sent him an essay of some forty thousand words which has been given the name of a 'Project for a Scientific Psychology'. This essay was composed in 1895, at what might be described as the water-shed of Freud's career, when he was reluctantly moving from physiology to psychology; it is an attempt to state the facts of psychology in purely neurological terms. This paper and all the rest of Freud's communications to Fliess have, by a lucky chance, survived: they throw a fascinating light on the development of Freud's ideas and show how much of the later findings of psycho-analysis were already present in his mind at this early stage.

Apart from his relations with Fliess, Freud had little outside support to begin with. He gradually gathered a few pupils round him in Vienna, but it was only after some ten years, in about 1906, that a change was inaugurated by the adhesion of a number of Swiss psychiatrists to his views. Chief among these were Bleuler, the head of the Zürich mental hospital, and his assistant Jung. This proved to be the beginning of the first spread of psycho-analysis. An international meeting of psycho-analysts gathered at Salzburg in 1908, and in 1909 Freud and Jung were invited to give a number of lectures in the United States. Freud's writings began to be translated into many languages, and groups of practising analysts sprang up all over the world. But the progress of psycho-analysis was not without its set-backs: the currents which its subject-matter stirred up in the mind ran too deep for its easy acceptance. In 1911 one of Freud's prominent Viennese supporters, Alfred Adler, broke away from him, and two or three years later Jung's differences from Freud led to their separation. Almost immediately after this came the First World War and an interruption of the international spread of psycho-analysis. Soon afterwards, too, came the gravest personal tragedies – the death of a daughter and of a favourite grandchild, and the onset of the malignant illness which was to pursue him relentlessly for the last sixteen years of his life. None of these troubles, however, brought any interruption to the development of Freud's observations and inferences. The structure of his ideas continued to expand and to find ever wider applications – particularly in the sociological field. By now he had become generally recognized as a figure of world celebrity, and no honour pleased him more than his election in 1936, the year of his eightieth birthday, as a Corresponding Member of the Royal Society. It was no doubt this fame, supported by the efforts of influential admirers, including, it is said, President Roosevelt, that protected him from the worst excesses of the National Socialists when Hitler invaded Austria in 1938, though they seized and destroyed his publications. Freud's departure from Vienna was nevertheless essential, and in June of that year, accompanied by some of his family, he made the journey to London, and it was there, a year later, on 23 September 1939, that he died.

*

It has become a journalistic cliché to speak of Freud as one of the revolutionary founders of modern thought and to couple his name with that of Einstein. Most people would however find it almost as hard to summarize the changes introduced by the one as by the other.

Freud's discoveries may be grouped under three headings – an instrument of research, the findings produced by the instrument, and the theoretical hypotheses inferred from the findings – though the three groups were of course mutually interrelated. Behind all of Freud's work, however, we should posit his belief in the universal validity of the law of determinism. As regards physical phenomena this belief

was perhaps derived from his experience in Brücke's laboratory and so, ultimately, from the school of Helmholz; but
Freud extended the belief uncompromisingly to the field
of mental phenomena, and here he may have been influenced by his teacher, the psychiatrist Meynert, and indir-
ectly by the philosophy of Herbart.

First and foremost, Freud was the discoverer of the first
instrument for the scientific examination of the human
mind. Creative writers of genius had had fragmentary insight into mental processes, but no systematic method of
investigation existed before Freud. It was only gradually
that he perfected the instrument, since it was only gradually that the difficulties in the way of such an investigation
became apparent. The forgotten trauma in Breuer's explanation of hysteria provided the earliest problem and perhaps the most fundamental of all, for it showed conclusively
that there were active parts of the mind not immediately
open to inspection either by an onlooker or by the subject
himself. These parts of the mind were described by Freud,
without regard for metaphysical or terminological disputes,
as the unconscious. Their existence was equally demonstrated by the fact of post-hypnotic suggestion, where a
person in a fully waking state performs an action which
had been suggested to him some time earlier, though he had
totally forgotten the suggestion itself. No examination of
the mind could thus be considered complete unless it included this unconscious part of it in its scope. How was this
to be accomplished? The obvious answer seemed to be: by
means of hypnotic suggestion; and this was the instrument
used by Breuer and, to begin with, by Freud. But it soon
turned out to be an imperfect one, acting irregularly and
uncertainly and sometimes not at all. Little by little, accordingly, Freud abandoned the use of suggestion and replaced
it by an entirely fresh instrument, which was later known
as 'free association'. He adopted the unheard-of plan of
simply asking the person whose mind he was investigating

to say whatever came into his head. This crucial decision led at once to the most startling results; even in this primitive form Freud's instrument produced fresh insight. For, though things went along swimmingly for a while, sooner or later the flow of associations dried up: the subject would not or could not think of anything more to say. There thus came to light the fact of 'resistance', of a force, separate from the subject's conscious will, which was refusing to collaborate with the investigation. Here was one basis for a very fundamental piece of theory, for a hypothesis of the mind as something dynamic, as consisting in a number of mental forces, some conscious and some unconscious, operating now in harmony now in opposition with one another.

Though these phenomena eventually turned out to be of universal occurrence, they were first observed and studied in neurotic patients, and the earlier years of Freud's work were largely concerned with discovering means by which the 'resistance' of these patients could be overcome and what lay behind it could be brought to light. The solution was only made possible by an extraordinary piece of self-observation on Freud's part – what we should now describe as his self-analysis. We are fortunate in having a contemporary first-hand description of this event in his letters to Fliess which have already been mentioned. This analysis enabled him to discover the nature of the unconscious processes at work in the mind and to understand why there is such a strong resistance to their becoming conscious; it enabled him to devise techniques for overcoming or evading the resistance in his patients; and, most important of all, it enabled him to realize the very great difference between the mode of functioning of these unconscious processes and that of our familiar conscious ones. A word may be said on each of these three points, for in fact they constitute the core of Freud's contributions to our knowledge of the mind.

The unconscious contents of the mind were found to consist wholly in the activity of conative trends – desires or wishes – which derive their energy directly from the primary physical instincts. They function quite regardless of any consideration other than that of obtaining immediate satisfaction, and are thus liable to be out of step with those more conscious elements in the mind which are concerned with adaptation to reality and the avoidance of external dangers. Since, moreover, these primitive trends are to a great extent of a sexual or of a destructive nature, they are bound to come in conflict with the more social and civilized mental forces. Investigations along this path were what led Freud to his discoveries of the long-disguised secrets of the sexual life of children and of the Oedipus complex.

In the second place, his self-analysis led him to an inquiry into the nature of dreams. These turned out to be, like neurotic symptoms, the product of a conflict and a compromise between the primary unconscious impulses and the secondary conscious ones. By analysing them into their elements it was therefore possible to infer their hidden unconscious contents; and, since dreams are common phenomena of almost universal occurrence, their interpretation turned out to be one of the most useful technical contrivances for penetrating the resistances of neurotic patients.

Finally, the painstaking examination of dreams enabled Freud to classify the remarkable differences between what he termed the primary and secondary processes of thought, between events in the unconscious and conscious regions of the mind. In the unconscious, it was found, there is no sort of organization or coordination: each separate impulse seeks satisfaction independently of all the rest; they proceed uninfluenced by one another; contradictions are completely inoperative, and the most opposite impulses flourish side by side. So. too, in the unconscious, associations of ideas proceed along lines without any regard to logic: similarities are treated as identities, negatives are equated with positives. Again, the objects to which the conative trends are attached in the unconscious are extraordinarily changeable – one may be replaced by another along a whole chain of associations that have no rational basis. Freud perceived that the intrusion into conscious thinking of mechanisms that belong properly to the primary process accounts for the oddity not only of dreams but of many other normal and pathological mental events.

It is not much of an exaggeration to say that all the later part of Freud's work lay in an immense extension and elaboration of these early ideas. They were applied to an elucidation of the mechanisms not only of the psycho-neuroses and psychoses but also of such normal processes as slips of the tongue, making jokes, artistic creation, political institutions, and religions; they played a part in throwing fresh light on many applied sciences – archaeology, anthropology, criminology, education; they also served to account for the effectiveness of psycho-analytic therapy. Lastly, too, Freud erected on the basis of these elementary observations a theoretical superstructure, what he named a 'metapsychology', of more general concepts. These, however, fascinating as many people will find them, he always insisted were in the nature of provisional hypotheses. Quite late in his life, indeed, influenced by the ambiguity of the term 'unconscious' and its many conflicting uses, he proposed a new structural account of the mind in which the uncoordinated instinctual trends were called the 'id', the organized realistic part the 'ego', and the critical and moral-izing function the 'super-ego' – a new account which has certainly made for a clarification of many issues.

*

This, then, will have given the reader an outline of the ex-ternal events of Freud's life and some notion of the scope of his discoveries. Is it legitimate to ask for more? to try to penetrate a little further and to inquire what sort of per-son Freud was? Possibly not. But human curiosity about great men is insatiable, and if it is not gratified with true accounts it will inevitably clutch at mythological ones. In two of Freud's early books (*The Interpretation of Dreams* and *The Psychopathology of Everyday Life*) the presentation of his thesis had forced on him the necessity of bringing up an unusual amount of personal material. Nevertheless, or perhaps for that very reason, he intensely objected to any intrusion into his private life, and he was correspondingly the subject of a wealth of myths. According to the first and most naïve rumours, for instance, he was an abandoned profligate, devoted to the corruption of public morals. Later fantasies have tended in the opposite direction: he has been represented as a harsh moralist, a ruthless disciplinarian, an autocrat, egocentric and unsmiling, and an essentially unhappy man. To anyone who was acquainted with him, even slightly, both these pictures must seem equally preposterous. The second of them was no doubt partly derived from a knowledge of his physical sufferings during his last years; but partly too it may have been due to the unfortunate impression produced by some of his most widespread portraits. He disliked being photographed, at least by professional photographers, and his features on occasion expressed the fact; artists too seem always to have been overwhelmed by the necessity for representing the inventor of psycho-analysis as a ferocious and terrifying figure. Fortunately, however, alternative versions exist of a more amiable and truer kind – snapshots, for instance, taken on a holiday or with his children, such as will be found in his eldest son's memoir of his father (*Glory Reflected*, by Martin Freud). In many ways, indeed, this delightful and amusing book serves to redress the balance from more official biographies, invaluable as they are, and reveals something of Freud as he was in ordinary life. Some of these portraits show us that in his earlier days he had well-filled features, but in later life, at any rate after the First World War and even before his illness, this was no longer so, and his features, as well as his whole figure (which was of medium height), were chiefly remarkable for the impression they gave of tense energy and alert observation. He was serious but kindly and considerate in his more formal manners, but in other circumstances could be an entertaining talker with a pleasantly ironical sense of humour. It was easy to discover his devoted fondness for his family and to recognize a man who would inspire affection. He had many miscellaneous interests – he was fond of travelling abroad, of country holidays, of mountain walks – and there were other, more engrossing subjects, art, archaeology, literature. Freud was a very well-read man in many languages, not only in German. He read English and French fluently, besides having a fair knowledge of Spanish and Italian. It must be remembered, too, that though the later phases of his education were chiefly scientific (it is true that at the University he studied philosophy for a short time) at school he had learnt the classics and never lost his affection for them. We happen to have a letter written by him at the age of seventeen to a school friend. In it he describes his varying success in the different papers of his school-leaving examination: in Latin a passage from Virgil, and in Greek thirty-three lines from, of all things, *Oedipus Rex*.

In short, we might regard Freud as what in England we should consider the best kind of product of a Victorian upbringing. His tastes in literature and art would obviously differ from ours, his views on ethics, though decidedly liberal, would not belong to the post-Freudian age. But we should see in him a man who lived a life of full emotion and of much suffering without embitterment. Complete honesty and directness were qualities that stood out in him, and so too did his intellectual readiness to take in and consider any fact, however new or extraordinary, that was presented to him. It was perhaps an inevitable corollary and extension of these qualities, combined with a general benevolence which a surface misanthropy failed to disguise, that led to some features of a surprising kind. In spite of his subtlety of mind he was essentially unsophisticated, and there were sometimes unexpected lapses in his critical faculty – a failure, for instance, to perceive an untrustworthy authority in some subject that was off his own beat such as Egyptology or philology, and, strangest of all in someone whose powers of perception had to be experienced to be believed, an occasional blindness to defects in his acquaintances. But though it may flatter our vanity to declare that Freud was a human being of a kind like our own, that satisfaction can easily be carried too far. There must in fact have been something very extraordinary in the man who was first able to recognize a whole field of mental facts which had hitherto been excluded from normal consciousness, the man who first interpreted dreams, who first accepted the facts of infantile sexuality, who first made the distinction between the primary and secondary processes of thinking – the man who first made the unconscious mind real to us.

*

Those in search of further information will find it in Ernest Jones's biography of Freud, in the collection of his letters edited by his son, Ernst Freud, and in the many volumes of the Standard Edition of his complete psychological works.

CHRONOLOGICAL TABLE

This table traces very roughly some of the main turning-points in Freud's intellectual development and opinions. A few of the chief events in his external life are also included in it.

1856. 6 May. Birth at Freiberg in Moravia

1860. Family settles in Vienna.

1865. Enters Gymnasium (secondary school).

1873. Enters Vienna University as medical student.

1876–82. Works under Brücke at the Institute of Physiology in Vienna.

1877. First publications: papers on anatomy and physiology.

1881. Graduates as Doctor of Medicine.

1882. Engagement to Martha Bernays.

1882–5. Works in Vienna General Hospital, concentrating on cerebral anatomy: numerous publications.

1884–7. Researches into the clinical uses of cocaine.

1885. Appointed *Privatdozent* (University Lecturer) in Neuropathology.

1885 (October)–1886 (February). Studies under Charcot at the Salpêtrière (hospital for nervous diseases) in Paris. Interest first turns to hysteria and hypnosis.

1886. Marriage to Martha Bernays. Sets up private practice in nervous diseases in Vienna.

1886–93. Continues work on neurology, especially on the cerebral palsies of children at the Kassowitz Institute in Vienna, with numerous publications. Gradual shift of interest from neurology to psychopathology.

1887. Birth of eldest child (Mathilde).

1887–1902. Friendship and correspondence with Wilhelm Fliess in Berlin. Freud's letters to him during this period, published posthumously in 1950, throw much light on the development of his views.

1887. Begins the use of hypnotic suggestion in his practice.

c. 1888. Begins to follow Breuer in using hypnosis for cathartic treatment of hysteria. Gradually drops hypnosis and substitutes free association.

1889. Visits Bernheim at Nancy to study his suggestion technique.

1889. Birth of eldest son (Martin).

1891. Monograph on Aphasia.
Birth of second son (Oliver).

1892. Birth of youngest son (Ernst).

1893. Publication of Breuer and Freud 'Preliminary Communication': exposition of trauma theory of hysteria and of cathartic treatment.
Birth of second daughter (Sophie).

1893–8. Researches and short papers on hysteria, obsessions, and anxiety.

1895. Jointly with Breuer, *Studies on Hysteria*: case histories and description by Freud of his technique, including first account of transference.

1893–6. Gradual divergence of views between Freud and Breuer. Freud introduces concepts of defence and repression and of neurosis being a result of a conflict between the ego and the libido.

1895. *Project for a Scientific Psychology*: included in Freud's letters to Fliess and first published in 1950. An abortive attempt to state psychology in neurological terms; but foreshadows much of Freud's later theories.
Birth of youngest child (Anna).

1896. Introduces the term 'psycho-analysis'.
Death of father (aged 80).

1897. Freud's self-analysis, leading to the abandonment of the trauma theory and the recognition of infantile sexuality and the Oedipus complex.

1900. *The Interpretation of Dreams*, with final chapter giving first full account of Freud's dynamic view of mental processes, of the unconscious, and of the dominance of the 'pleasure principle'.

1901. *The Psychopathology of Everyday Life*. This, together with the book on dreams, made it plain that Freud's theories applied not only to pathological states but also to normal mental life.

1902. Appointed Professor Extraordinarius.

1905. *Three Essays on the Theory of Sexuality* : tracing for the first time the course of development of the sexual instinct in human beings from infancy to maturity.

c. 1906. Jung becomes an adherent of psycho-analysis.

1908. First international meeting of psycho-analysts (at Salzburg).

1909. Freud and Jung invited to the U.S.A. to lecture.

Case history of the first analysis of a child (Little Hans, aged five) : confirming inferences previously made from adult analyses, especially as to infantile sexuality and the Oedipus and castration complexes.

c. 1910. First emergence of the theory of 'narcissism'.

1911–15. Papers on the technique of psycho-analysis.

1911. Secession of Adler.

Application of psycho-analytic theories to a psychotic case : the autobiography of Dr Schreber.

1913–14. *Totem and Taboo* : application of psycho-analysis to anthropological material.

1914. Secession of Jung.

'On the History of the Psycho-Analytic Movement'. Includes a polemical section on Adler and Jung.

Writes his last major case history, of the 'Wolf Man' (not published till 1918).

1915. Writes a series of twelve 'metapsychological' papers on basic theoretical questions, of which only five have survived.

1915–17. *Introductory Lectures* : giving an extensive general account of the state of Freud's views up to the time of the First World War.

1919. Application of the theory of narcissism to the war neuroses.

1920. Death of second daughter.

Beyond the Pleasure Principle ; the first explicit introduction of the concept of the 'compulsion to repeat' and of the theory of the 'death instinct'.

1921. *Group Psychology*. Beginnings of a systematic analytic study of the ego.

1923. *The Ego and the Id*. Largely revised account of the

structure and functioning of the mind with the division into an id, an ego, and a super-ego.

1923. First onset of cancer.

1925. Revised views on the sexual development of women.

1926. *Inhibitions, Symptoms, and Anxiety*. Revised views on the problem of anxiety.

1927. *The Future of an Illusion*. A discussion of religion: the first of a number of sociological works to which Freud devoted most of his remaining years.

1930. *Civilization and it Discontents*. This includes Freud's first extensive study of the destructive instinct (regarded as a manifestation of the 'death instinct').
Freud awarded the Goethe Prize by the City of Frankfurt.
Death of mother (aged ninety-five).

1933. Hitler seizes power in Germany: Freud's books publicly burned in Berlin.

1934-8. *Moses and Monotheism*: the last of Freud's works to appear during his lifetime.

1936. Eightieth birthday. Election as Corresponding Member of Royal Society.

1938. Hitler's invasion of Austria. Freud leaves Vienna for London.
An Outline of Psycho-Analysis. A final, unfinished, but profound, exposition of psycho-analysis.

1939. 23 September. Death in London.

FIVE LECTURES ON PSYCHO-ANALYSIS

*Delivered on the Occasion of the Celebration of the
Twentieth Anniversary of the Foundation of
Clark University, Worcester, Massachusetts,
September 1909*

FIRST LECTURE

LADIES AND GENTLEMEN, It is with novel and bewildering feelings that I find myself in the New World, lecturing before an audience of expectant inquirers. No doubt I owe this honour only to the fact that my name is linked with the topic of psycho-analysis; and it is of psycho-analysis, therefore, that I intend to speak to you. I shall attempt to give you, as succinctly as possible, a survey of the history and subsequent development of this new method of examination and treatment.

If it is a merit to have brought psycho-analysis into being, that merit is not mine.* I had no share in its earliest beginnings. I was a student and working for my final examinations at the time when another Viennese physician, Dr Josef Breuer,† first (in 1880-2) made use of this procedure on a girl who was suffering from hysteria. Let us turn our attention straightaway to the history of this case and its treatment, which you will find set out in detail in the *Studies on Hysteria* [1895]‡ which were published later by Breuer and myself.

* (*Footnote added* 1923) See, however, in this connexion my remarks in 'A History of the Psycho-Analytic Movement' (1914), where I assumed the entire responsibilty for psycho-analysis.

† Dr Josef Breuer, born in 1842, a Corresponding Member of the Kaiserliche Akademie der Wissenschaften [Imperial Academy of Sciences], is well known for his work on respiration and on the physiology of the sense of equilibrium. [His obituary by Freud (1925) included a more detailed account of his career.]

‡ Some of my contributions to this book have been translated into English by Dr A. A. Brill of New York : *Selected Papers on Hysteria* (New York, 1909). [A new translation of the whole book appeared in 1955, where the case history of this patient (Fraulein Anna O.) will be found on p. 21 ff.]

But I should like to make one preliminary remark. It is not without satisfaction that I have learnt that the majority of my audience are not members of the medical profession. You have no need to be afraid that any special medical knowledge will be required for following what I have to say. It is true that we shall go along with the doctors on the first stage of our journey, but we shall soon part company with them and, with Dr Breuer, shall pursue a quite individual path.

Dr Breuer's patient was a girl of twenty-one, of high intellectual gifts. Her illness lasted for over two years, and in the course of it she developed a series of physical and psychological disturbances which decidedly deserved to be taken seriously. She suffered from a rigid paralysis, accompanied by loss of sensation, of both extremities on the right side of her body; and the same trouble from time to time affected her on her left side. Her eye movements were disturbed and her power of vision was subject to numerous restrictions. She had difficulties over the posture of her head; she had a severe nervous cough. She had an aversion to taking nourishment, and on one occasion she was for several weeks unable to drink in spite of a tormenting thirst. Her powers of speech were reduced, even to the point of her being unable to speak or understand her native language. Finally, she was subject to conditions of '*absence*',* of confusion, of delirium, and of alteration of her whole personality, to which we shall have presently to turn our attention.

When you hear such an enumeration of symptoms, you will be inclined to think it safe to assume, even though you are not doctors, that what we have before us is a severe illness, probably affecting the brain, that it offers small prospect of recovery and will probably lead to the patient's early decease. You must be prepared to learn from the doctors, however, that, in a number of cases which display

*[The French term.]

severe symptoms such as these, it is justifiable to take a different and a far more favourable view. If a picture of this kind is presented by a young patient of the female sex, whose vital internal organs (heart, kidneys, etc.) are shown on objective examination to be normal, but who has been subjected to violent *emotional* shocks – if, moreover, her various symptoms differ in certain matters of detail from what would have been expected – then doctors are not inclined to take the case too seriously. They decide that what they have before them is not an organic disease of the brain, but the enigmatic condition which from the time of ancient Greek medicine has been known as 'hysteria' and which has the power of producing illusory pictures of a whole number of serious diseases. They consider that there is then no risk to life but that a return to health – even a complete one – is probable. It is not always quite easy to distinguish a hysteria like this from a severe organic illness. There is no need for us to know, however, how a differential diagnosis of that kind is made; it will suffice to have an assurance that the case of Breuer's patient was precisely of a kind in which no competent physician could fail to make a diagnosis of hysteria. And here we may quote from the report of the patient's illness the further fact that it made its appearance at a time when she was nursing her father, of whom she was devotedly fond, through the grave illness which led to his death, and that, as a result of her own illness, she was obliged to give up nursing him.

So far it has been an advantage to us to accompany the doctors; but the moment of parting is at hand. For you must not suppose that a patient's prospects of medical assistance are improved in essentials by the fact that a diagnosis of hysteria has been substituted for one of severe organic disease of the brain. Medical skill is in most cases powerless against severe diseases of the brain; but neither can the doctor do anything against hysterical disorders. He must

leave it to kindly Nature to decide when and how his optim-
istic prognosis shall be fulfilled.*

Thus the recognition of the illness as hysteria makes little
difference to the patient; but to the doctor quite the reverse.
It is noticeable that his attitude towards hysterical patients
is quite other than towards sufferers from organic diseases.
He does not have the same sympathy for the former as for
the latter : for the hysteric's ailment is in fact far less serious
and yet it seems to claim to be regarded as equally so. And
there is a further factor at work. Through his studies, the
doctor has learnt many things that remain a sealed book to
the layman : he has been able to form ideas on the causes of
illness and on the changes it brings about – e.g., in the brain
of a person suffering from apoplexy or from a malignant
growth – ideas which must to some degree meet the case.
since they allow him to understand the details of the illness.
But all his knowledge – his training in anatomy, in physiology, and in pathology – leaves him in the lurch when he is
confronted by the details of hysterical phenomena. He cannot understand hysteria, and in the face of it he is himself a
layman. This is not a pleasant situation for anyone who
as a rule sets so much store by his knowledge. So it comes
about that hysterical patients forfeit his sympathy. He
regards them as people who are transgressing the laws of his
science – like heretics in the eyes of the orthodox. He
attributes every kind of wickedness to them, accuses them
of exaggeration, of deliberate deceit, of malingering.
And he punishes them by withdrawing his interest from
them.

Dr Breuer's attitude towards his patient deserved no such
reproach. He gave her both sympathy and interest, even
though, to begin with, he did not know how to help her. It

---

*I am aware that this is no longer the case; but in my lecture I
am putting myself and my hearers back into the period before 1880.
If things are different now, that is to a great extent the result of the
activities whose history I am now sketching.

seems likely that she herself made his task easier by the admirable qualities of intellect and character to which he has testified in her case history. Soon, moreover, his benevolent scrutiny showed him the means of bringing her a first instalment of help.

It was observed that, while the patient was in her states of *'absence'* (altered personality accompanied by confusion), she was in the habit of muttering a few words to herself which seemed as though they arose from some train of thought that was occupying her mind. The doctor, after getting a report of these words, used to put her into a kind of hypnosis and then repeat them to her so as to induce her to use them as a starting-point. The patient complied with the plan, and in this way reproduced in his presence the mental creations which had been occupying her mind during the *'absences'* and which had betrayed their existence by the fragmentary words which she had uttered. They were profoundly melancholy phantasies – 'daydreams' we should call them – sometimes characterized by poetic beauty, and their starting-point was as a rule the position of a girl at her father's sick-bed. When she had related a number of these phantasies, she was as if set free, and she was brought back to normal mental life. The improvement in her condition, which would last for several hours, would be succeeded next day by a further attack of *'absence'*; and this in turn would be removed in the same way by getting her to put into words her freshly constructed phantasies. It was impossible to escape the conclusion that the alteration in her mental state which was expressed in the *'absences'* was a result of the stimulus proceeding from these highly emotional phantasies. The patient herself, who, strange to say, could at this time only speak and understand English, christened this novel kind of treatment the 'talking cure' or used to refer to it jokingly as 'chimney-sweeping'.

It soon emerged, as though by chance, that this process of sweeping the mind clean could accomplish more than the merely temporary relief of her ever-recurring mental confusion. It was actually possible to bring about the disappearance of the painful symptoms of her illness, if she could be brought to remember under hypnosis, with an accompanying expression of affect, on what occasion and in what connexion the symptoms had first appeared. 'It was in the summer during a period of extreme heat, and the patient was suffering very badly from thirst; for, without being able to account for it in any way, she suddenly found it impossible to drink. She would take up the glass of water that she longed for, but as soon as it touched her lips she would push it away like someone suffering from hydrophobia. As she did this, she was obviously in an *"absence"* for a couple of seconds. She lived only on fruit, such as melons, etc., so as to lessen her tormenting thirst. This had lasted for some six weeks, when one day during hypnosis she grumbled about her English "lady-companion", whom she did not care for, and went on to describe, with every sign of disgust, how she had once gone into this lady's room and how her little dog – horrid creature! – had drunk out of a glass there. The patient had said nothing, as she had wanted to be polite. After giving further energetic expression to the anger she had held back, she asked for something to drink, drank a large quantity of water without any difficulty, and awoke from her hypnosis with the glass at her lips; and thereupon the disturbance vanished, never to return.' *

With your permission, I should like to pause a moment over this event. Never before had anyone removed a hysterical symptom by such a method or had thus gained so deep an insight into its causation. It could not fail to prove a momentous discovery if the expectation were confirmed that others of the patient's symptoms – perhaps the majority of them – had arisen and could be removed in this same manner. Breuer spared no pains in convincing himself that this was so, and he proceeded to a systematic investigation

* *Studies on Hysteria* [p. 34].

of the pathogenesis of the other and more serious symptoms of the patient's illness. And it really *was* so. Almost all the symptoms had arisen in this way as residues – 'precipitates' they might be called – of emotional experiences. To these experiences, therefore, we later gave the name of 'psychical traumas', while the particular nature of the symptoms was explained by their relation to the traumatic scenes which were their cause. They were, to use a technical term, 'determined' by the scenes of whose recollection they represented residues, and it was no longer necessary to describe them as capricious or enigmatic products of the neurosis. One unexpected point, however, must be noticed. What left the symptom behind was not always a *single* experience. On the contrary, the result was usually brought about by the convergence of several traumas, and often by the repetition of a great number of similar ones. Thus it was necessary to reproduce the whole chain of pathogenic memories in chronological order, or rather in reversed order, the latest ones first and the earliest ones last; and it was quite impossible to jump over the later traumas in order to get back more quickly to the first, which was often the most potent one.

No doubt you will now ask me for some further instances of the causation of hysterical symptoms besides the one I have already given you of a fear of water produced by disgust at a dog drinking out of a glass. But if I am to keep to my programme I shall have to restrict myself to very few examples. In regard to the patient's disturbances of vision, for instance, Breuer describes how they were traced back to occasions such as one on which, 'when she was sitting by her father's bedside with tears in her eyes, he suddenly asked her what time it was. She could not see clearly; she made a great effort, and brought her watch near to her eyes. The face of the watch now seemed very big – thus accounting for her macropsia and convergent squint. Or again, she tried hard to suppress her tears so that the sick man should not see them.' * Moreover, all of the pathogenic impressions came from the period during which she was helping to nurse her sick father. 'She once woke up during the night in great anxiety about the patient, who was in a high fever; and she was under the strain of expecting the arrival of a surgeon from Vienna who was to operate. Her mother had gone away for a short time and Anna was sitting at the bedside with her right arm over the back of her chair. She fell into a waking dream and saw a black snake coming towards the sick man from the wall to bite him. (It is most likely that there were in fact snakes in the field behind the house and that these had previously given the girl a fright; they would thus have provided the material for her hallucination.) She tried to keep the snake off, but it was as though she was paralysed. Her right arm over the back of the chair, had gone to sleep, and had become anaesthetic and paretic; and when she looked at it the fingers turned into little snakes with death's heads (the nails). (It seems probable that she had tried to use her paralysed right hand to drive off the snake and that its anaesthesia and paralysis had consequently become associated with the hallucination of the snake.) When the snake vanished, in her terror she tried to pray. But language failed her: she could find no tongue in which to speak, till at last she thought of some children's verses in English and then found herself able to think and pray in that language.'† When the patient had recollected this scene in hypnosis, the rigid paralysis of her right arm, which had persisted since the beginning of her illness, disappeared, and the treatment was brought to an end.

When, some years later, I began to employ Breuer's method of examination and treatment on patients of my own, my experiences agreed entirely with his. A lady, aged about forty, suffered from a *tic* consisting of a peculiar 'clacking' sound which she produced whenever she was excited, or

* *Studies on Hysteria* [pp. 39–40].
† *Studies on Hysteria* [pp. 38–9].

sometimes for no visible reason. It had its origin in two experiences, whose common element lay in the fact that at
the moment of their occurrence she had formed a determination not to make any noise, and in the fact that on both
these occasions a kind of counter-will led her to break the
silence with this same sound. On the first of these occasions
one of her children had been ill, and, when she had at last
with great difficulty succeeded in getting it off to sleep, she
had said to herself that she must keep absolutely still so as
not to wake it. On the other occasion, while she was driving
with her two children in a thunderstorm, the horses had
bolted and she had carefully tried to avoid making any
noise for fear of frightening them even more.* I give you
this one example out of a number of others which are reported in the *Studies on Hysteria*.†

Ladies and Gentlemen, if I may be allowed to generalize –
which is unavoidable in so condensed an account as this – I
should like to formulate what we have learned so far as follows: *our hysterical patients suffer from reminiscences.*
Their symptoms are residues and mnemic symbols of particular (traumatic) experiences. We may perhaps obtain a
deeper understanding of this kind of symbolism if we com-
pare them with other mnemic symbols in other fields. The
monuments and memorials with which large cities are
adorned are also mnemic symbols. If you take a walk
through the streets of London, you will find, in front of one
of the great railway termini, a richly carved Gothic column
– Charing Cross. One of the old Plantagenet kings of the
thirteenth century ordered the body of his beloved Queen
Eleanor to be carried to Westminster; and at every stage at
which the coffin rested he erected a Gothic cross. Charing
Cross is the last of the monuments that commemorate the

* *Studies on Hysteria* [pp. 54 and 58].
† The case here reported is that of Frau Emmy von N., the second
in *Studies on Hysteria*, [pp. 48-9].

funeral cortège.* At another point in the same town, not far from London Bridge, you will find a towering, and more modern, column, which is simply known as 'The Monument'. It was designed as a memorial of the Great Fire, which broke out in that neighbourhood in 1666 and destroyed a large part of the city. These monuments, then, resemble hysterical symptoms in being mnemic symbols; up to that point the comparison seems justifiable. But what should we think of a Londoner who paused today in deep melancholy before the memorial of Queen Eleanor's funeral instead of going about his business in the hurry that modern working conditions demand or instead of feeling joy over the youthful queen of his own heart? Or again what should we think of a Londoner who shed tears before the Monument that commemorates the reduction of his beloved metropolis to ashes although it has long since risen again in far greater brilliance? Yet every single hysteric and neurotic behaves like these two unpractical Londoners. Not only do they remember painful experiences of the remote past, but they still cling to them emotionally; they cannot get free of the past and for its sake they neglect what is real and immediate. This fixation of mental life to pathogenic traumas is one of the most significant and practically important characteristics of neurosis.

I am quite ready to allow the justice of an objection that you are probably raising at this moment on the basis of the case history of Breuer's patient. It is quite true that all her traumas dated from the period when she was nursing her sick father and that her symptoms can only be regarded as mnemic signs of his illness and death. Thus they correspond to a display of mourning, and there is certainly nothing pathological in being fixated to the memory of a dead person so short a time after his decease; on the contrary, it would

* Or rather, it is a modern copy of one of these monuments. As Dr Ernest Jones tells me, the name 'Charing' is believed to be derived from the words 'chère reine'.

be a normal emotional process. I grant you that in the case of Breuer's patient there is nothing striking in her fixation to her trauma. But in other cases – such as that of the *tic* that I treated myself, where the determinants dated back more than fifteen and ten years – the feature of an abnormal attachment to the past is very clear; and it seems likely that Breuer's patient would have developed a similar feature if she had not received cathartic treatment so soon after experiencing the traumas and developing the symptoms.

So far we have only been discussing the relations between a patient's hysterical symptoms and the events of her life. There are, however, two further factors in Breuer's observation which enable us to form some notion of how the processes of falling ill and of recovering occur.

In the first place, it must be emphasized that Breuer's patient, in almost all her pathogenic situations, was obliged to *suppress* a powerful emotion instead of allowing its discharge in the appropriate signs of emotion, words or actions. In the episode of her lady-companion's dog, she suppressed any manifestation of her very intense disgust, out of consideration for the woman's feelings; while she watched at her father's bedside she was constantly on the alert to prevent the sick man from observing her anxiety and her painful depression. When subsequently she reproduced these scenes in her doctor's presence the affect which had been inhibited at the time emerged with peculiar violence, as though it had been saved up for a long time. Indeed, the symptom which was left over from one of these scenes would reach its highest pitch of intensity at the time when its determining cause was being approached, only to vanish when that cause had been fully ventilated. On the other hand, it was found that no result was produced by the recollection of a scene in the doctor's presence if for some reason the recollection took place without any generation of affect. Thus it was what happened to these affects, which might be regarded as displaceable magnitudes [of energy], that was the decisive factor both for the onset of illness and for recovery. One was driven to assume that the illness occurred because the affects generated in the pathogenic situations had their normal outlet blocked, and that the essence of the illness lay in the fact that these 'strangulated' affects were then put to an abnormal use. In part they remained as a permanent burden upon the patient's mental life and a source of constant excitation for it; and in part they underwent a transformation into unusual somatic innervations and inhibitions, which manifested themselves as the physical symptoms of the case. For this latter process we coined the term 'hysterical conversion'. Quite apart from this, a certain portion of our mental excitation is normally directed along the paths of somatic innervation and produces what we know as an 'expression of the emotions'. Hysterical conversion exaggerates this portion of the discharge of an emotionally cathected [charged] mental process; it represents a far more intense expression of the emotions, which has entered upon a new path. When the bed of a stream is divided into two channels, then, if the current in one of them is brought up against an obstacle, the other will at once be overfilled. As you see, we are on the point of arriving at a purely psychological theory of hysteria, with affective processes in the front rank.

A second observation of Breuer's, again, compels us to attach great importance, among the characteristics of the pathological chain of events, to states of consciousness. Breuer's patient exhibited, alongside of her normal state, a number of mental peculiarities: conditions of '*absence*', confusion, and alterations of character. In her normal state she knew nothing of the pathogenic scenes or their connexion with her symptoms; she had forgotten the scenes, or at all events had severed the pathogenic link. When she was put under hypnosis, it was possible, at the expense of a considerable amount of labour, to recall the scenes to her memory; and through this work of recollecting, the symptoms were removed. The explanation of this fact would be a most awkward business, were it not that the way is pointed by experiences and experiments in hypnotism. The study of hypnotic phenomena has accustomed us to what was at first a bewildering realization that in one and the same individual there can be several mental groupings, which can remain more or less independent of one another, which can 'know nothing' of one another, and which can alternate with one another in their hold upon consciousness. Cases of this kind, too, occasionally appear spontaneously, and are then described as examples of '*double conscience*'.* If, where a splitting of the personality such as this has occurred, consciousness remains attached regularly to one of the two states, we call it the *conscious*† mental state and the other, which is detached from it, the *unconscious* one. In the familiar condition known as 'post-hypnotic suggestion', a command given under hypnosis is slavishly carried out subsequently in the normal state. This phenomenon affords an admirable example of the influences which the unconscious state can exercise over the conscious one; moreover, it provides a pattern upon which we can account for the phenomena of hysteria. Breuer adopted a hypothesis that hysterical symptoms arise in peculiar mental conditions to which he gave the name of 'hypnoid'. On this view, excitations occurring during these hypnoid states can easily become pathogenic because such states do not provide opportunities for the normal discharge of the process of excitation. There consequently arises from the process of excitation an unusual product – the symptom. This finds its way, like a foreign body, into the normal state, which in turn is in ignorance of the hypnoid pathogenic situation. Wherever there is a symptom there is also an amnesia, a

* [The French term for 'dual consciousness'.]
† [See some remarks on Freud's use of this word in a footnote on pp. 107 below.]

gap in the memory, and filling up this gap implies the removal of the conditions which led to the production of the symptom.

This last part of my account will not, I fear, strike you as particularly clear. But you should bear in mind that we are dealing with novel and difficult considerations, and it may well be that it is not possible to make them much clearer – which shows that we still have a long way to go in our knowledge of the subject. Moreover, Breuer's theory of 'hypnoid states' turned out to be impeding and unnecessary, and it has been dropped by psycho-analysis today. Later on, you will at least have a hint of the influences and processes that were to be discovered behind the screen of hypnoid states erected by Breuer. You will have rightly formed the opinion, too, that Breuer's investigation has only succeeded in offering you a very incomplete theory and an unsatisfying explanation of the phenomena observed. But complete theories do not fall ready-made from the sky, and you would have even better grounds for suspicion if anyone presented you with a flawless and complete theory at the very beginning of his observations. Such a theory could only be a child of his speculation and could not be the fruit of an unprejudiced examination of the facts.

SECOND LECTURE

LADIES AND GENTLEMEN, At about the same time at which Breuer was carrying on the 'talking cure' with his patient, the great Charcot in Paris had begun the researches into hysterical patients at the Salpêtrière which were to lead to a new understanding of the disease. There was no possibility of his findings being known in Vienna at that time. But when, some ten years later, Breuer and I published our 'Preliminary Communication' on the psychical mechanism of hysterical phenomena [1893], we were completely under the spell of Charcot's researches. We regarded the pathogenic experiences of our patients as psychical traumas, and equated them with the somatic traumas whose influence on hysterical paralyses had been established by Charcot; and Breuer's hypothesis of hypnoid states was itself nothing but a reflection of the fact that Charcot had reproduced those traumatic paralyses artificially under hypnosis.

The great French observer, whose pupil I became in 1885-6, was not himself inclined to adopt a psychological outlook. It was his pupil, Pierre Janet, who first attempted a deeper approach to the peculiar psychical processes present in hysteria, and we followed his example when we took the splitting of the mind and dissociation of the personality as the centre of our position. You will find in Janet a theory of hysteria which takes into account the prevailing views in France on the part played by heredity and degeneracy. According to him, hysteria is a form of degenerate modification of the nervous system, which shows itself in an innate weakness in the power of psychical synthesis. Hysterical patients, he believes, are inherently incapable of holding together the multiplicity of mental processes into a unity, and hence arises the tendency to mental dissociation. If I may be allowed to draw a homely but clear analogy, Janet's hysterical patient reminds one of a feeble woman who has gone out shopping and is now returning home laden with a multitude of parcels and boxes. She cannot contain the whole heap of them with her two arms and ten fingers. So first of all one object slips from her grasp; and when she stoops to pick it up, another one escapes her in its place, and so on. This supposed mental weakness of hysterical patients is not confirmed when we find that, alongside these phenomena of diminished capacity, examples are also to be observed of a partial increase in efficiency, as though by way of compensation. At the time when Breuer's patient had forgotten her mother tongue and every other language but English, her grasp of English reached such heights that, if she was handed a German book, she was able straight away to read out a correct and fluent translation of it.

When, later on, I set about continuing on my own account the investigations that had been begun by Breuer, I soon arrived at another view of the origin of hysterical dissociation (the splitting of consciousness). A divergence of this kind, which was to be decisive for everything that followed, was inevitable, since I did not start out, like Janet, from laboratory experiments, but with therapeutic aims in mind.

I was driven forward above all by practical necessity. The cathartic procedure, as carried out by Breuer, presupposed putting the patient into a state of deep hypnosis; for it was only in a state of hypnosis that he attained a knowledge of the pathogenic connexions which escaped him in his normal state. But I soon came to dislike hypnosis, for it was a temperamental and, one might almost say, a mystical ally. When I found that, in spite of all my efforts, I could not succeed in bringing more than a fraction of my patients into a hypnotic state, I determined to give up hypnosis and to make the cathartic procedure independent of it. Since I was not able at will to alter the mental state of the majority of my patients, I set about working with them in their *normal* state. At first, I must confess, this seemed a senseless and hopeless undertaking. I was set the task of learning from the patient something that I did not know and that he did not know himself. How could one hope to elicit it? But there came to my help a recollection of a most remarkable and instructive experiment which I had witnessed when I was with Bernheim at Nancy [in 1889]. Bernheim showed us that people whom he had put into a state of hypnotic somnambulism, and who had had all kinds of experiences while they were in that state, only *appeared* to have lost the memory of what they had experienced during somnambulism: it was possible to revive these memories in their normal state. It is true that, when he questioned them about their somnambulistic experiences, they began by maintaining that they knew nothing about them; but if he refused to give way, and insisted, and assured them that they *did* know about them, the forgotten experiences always reappeared.

So I did the same thing with my patients. When I reached a point with them at which they maintained that they knew nothing more, I assured them that they *did* know it all the same, and that they had only to say it; and I ventured to declare that the right memory would occur to them at the moment at which I laid my hand on their forehead. In that way I succeeded, without using hypnosis, in obtaining from the patients whatever was required for establishing the connexion between the pathogenic scenes they had forgotten and the symptoms left over from those scenes. But it was a laborious procedure, and in the long run an exhausting one; and it was unsuited to serve as a permanent technique.

I did not abandon it, however, before the observations I

made during my use of it afforded me decisive evidence. I found confirmation of the fact that the forgotten memories were not lost. They were in the patient's possession and were ready to emerge in association to what was still known by him; but there was some force that prevented them from becoming conscious and compelled them to remain unconscious. The existence of this force could be assumed with certainty, since one became aware of an effort corresponding to it if, in opposition to it, one tried to introduce the unconscious memories into the patient's consciousness. The force which was maintaining the pathological condition became apparent in the form of *resistance* on the part of the patient.

It was on this idea of resistance, then, that I based my view of the course of psychical events in hysteria. In order to effect a recovery, it had proved necessary to remove these resistances. Starting out from the mechanism of cure, it now became possible to construct quite definite ideas of the origin of the illness. The same forces which, in the form of resistance, were now offering opposition to the forgotten material's being made conscious, must formerly have brought about the forgetting and must have pushed the pathogenic experiences in question out of consciousness. I gave the name of *repression* to this hypothetical process, and I considered that it was proved by the undeniable existence of resistance.

The further question could then be raised as to what these forces were and what the determinants were of the repression in which we now recognized the pathogenic mechanism of hysteria. A comparative study of the pathogenic situations which we had come to know through the cathartic procedure made it possible to answer this question. All these experiences had involved the emergence of a wishful impulse which was in sharp contrast to the subject's other wishes and which proved incompatible with the ethical and aesthetic standards of his personalty. There had been a short conflict, and the end of this internal struggle was that the idea which had appeared before consciousness as the vehicle of this irreconcilable wish fell a victim to repression, was pushed out of consciousness with all its attached memories and was forgotten. Thus the incompatibility of the wish in question with the patient's ego was the motive for the repression; the subject's ethical and other standards were the repressing forces. An acceptance of the incompatible wishful impulse or a prolongation of the conflict would have produced a high degree of unpleasure; this unpleasure was avoided by means of repression, which was thus revealed as one of the devices serving to protect the mental personality.

To take the place of a number of instances, I will relate a single one of my cases, in which the determinants and advantages of repression are sufficiently evident. For my present purpose I shall have once again to abridge the case history and omit some important underlying material. The patient was a girl,* who had lost her beloved father after she had taken a share in nursing him – a situation analogous to that of Breuer's patient. Soon afterwards her elder sister married, and her new brother-in-law aroused in her a peculiar feeling of sympathy which was easily masked under a disguise of family affection. Not long afterwards her sister fell ill and died, in the absence of the patient and her mother. They were summoned in all haste without being given any definite information of the tragic event. When the girl reached the bedside of her dead sister, there came to her for a brief moment an idea that might be expressed in these words: 'Now he is free and can marry me.' We may assume with certainty that this idea, which betrayed to her consciousness the intense love for her brother-in-law of which she had not herself been conscious, was surrendered to repression a moment later, owing to the revolt of her feelings.

* [This is the case of Fräulein Elisabeth von R., the fifth of the case histories fully reported in *Studies on Hysteria*, p. 135 ff.]

The girl fell ill with severe hysterical symptoms; and while she was under my treatment it turned out that she had completely forgotten the scene by her sister's bedside and the odious egoistic impulse that had emerged in her. She remembered it during the treatment and reproduced the pathogenic moment with signs of the most violent emotion, and, as a result of the treatment, she became healthy once more.

Perhaps I may give you a more vivid picture of repression and of its necessary relation to resistance, by a rough analogy derived from our actual situation at the present moment. Let us suppose that in this lecture-room and among this audience, whose exemplary quiet and attentiveness I cannot sufficiently commend, there is nevertheless someone who is causing a disturbance and whose ill-mannered laughter, chattering, and shuffling with his feet are distracting my attention from my task. I have to announce that I cannot proceed with my lecture; and thereupon three or four of you who are strong men stand up and, after a short struggle, put the interrupter outside the door. So now he is 'repressed', and I can continue my lecture. But in order that the interruption shall not be repeated, in case the individual who has been expelled should try to enter the room once more, the gentlemen who have put my will into effect place their chairs up against the door and thus establish a 'resistance' after the repression has been accomplished. If you will now translate the two localities concerned into psychical terms as the 'conscious' and the 'unconscious', you will have before you a fairly good picture of the process of repression.

You will now see in what it is that the difference lies between our view and Janet's. We do not derive the psychical splitting from an innate incapacity for synthesis on the part of the mental apparatus; we explain it dynamically, from the conflict of opposing mental forces, and recognize it as the outcome of an active struggling on the part of the two psychical groupings against each other. But our view gives rise to a large number of fresh problems. Situations of mental conflict are, of course, exceedingly common; efforts by the ego to ward off painful memories are quite regularly to be observed without their producing the result of a mental split. The reflection cannot be escaped that further determinants must be present if the conflict is to lead to dissociation. I will also readily grant you that the hypothesis of repression leaves us not at the end but at the beginning of a psychological theory. We can only go forward step by step, however, and complete knowledge must await the results of further and deeper researches.

Nor is it advisable to attempt to explain the case of Breuer's patient from the point of view of repression. That case history is not suited to this purpose, because its findings were reached with the help of hypnotic influence. It is only if you exclude hypnosis that you can observe resistances and repressions and form an adequate idea of the truly pathogenic course of events. Hypnosis conceals the resistance and renders a certain area of the mind accessible; but, as against this, it builds up the resistance at the frontiers of this area into a wall that makes everything beyond it inaccessible.

Our most valuable lesson from Breuer's observation was what it proved concerning the relation between symptoms and pathogenic experiences or psychical traumas, and we must not omit now to consider these discoveries from the standpoint of the theory of repression. At first sight it really seems impossible to trace a path from repression to the formation of symptoms. Instead of giving a complicated theoretical account, I will return here to the analogy which I employed earlier for my explanation of repression. If you come to think of it, the removal of the interrupter and the posting of the guardians at the door may not mean the end of the story. It may very well be that the individual who has been expelled, and who has now become embittered and reckless, will cause us further trouble. It is true that he is no longer among us; we are free from his presence, from his insulting laughter and his *sotto voce* comments. But in some respects, nevertheless, the repression has been unsuccessful; for now he is making an intolerable exhibition of himself outside the room, and his shouting and banging on the door with his fists interfere with my lecture even more than his bad behaviour did before. In these circumstances we could not fail to be delighted if our respected president, Dr Stanley Hall, should be willing to assume the role of mediator and peacemaker. He would have a talk with the unruly person outside and would then come to us with a request that he should be re-admitted after all: he himself would guarantee that the man would now behave better. On Dr Hall's authority we decide to lift the repression, and peace and quiet are restored. This presents what is really no bad picture of the physician's task in the psycho-analytic treatment of the neuroses.

To put the matter more directly. The investigation of hysterical patients and of other neurotics leads us to the conclusion that their repression of the idea to which the intolerable wish is attached has been a *failure*. It is true that they have driven it out of consciousness and out of memory and have apparently saved themselves a large amount of unpleasure. *But the repressed wishful impulse continues to exist in the unconscious.* It is on the look-out for an opportunity of being activated, and when that happens it succeeds in sending into consciousness a disguised and unrecognizable *substitute* for what has been repressed, and to this there soon become attached the same feelings of unpleasure which it was hoped had been saved by the repression. This substitute for the repressed idea – the *symptom* – is proof against further attacks from the defensive ego; and in place of the short conflict an ailment now appears which is not brought to an end by the passage of time. Alongside the indication of distortion in the symptom, we can trace in it the remains of some kind of indirect resemblance to the idea that was originally repressed. The paths along which the substitution was effected can be traced in the course of the patient's psycho-analytic treatment; and in order to bring about recovery, the symptom must be led back along the same paths and once more turned into the repressed idea. If what was repressed is brought back again into conscious mental activity – a process which presupposes the overcoming of considerable resistances – the resulting psychical conflict, which the patient had tried to avoid, can, under the physician's guidance, reach a better outcome than was offered by repression. There are a number of such opportune solutions, which may bring the conflict and the neurosis to a happy end, and which may in certain instances be combined. The patient's personality may be convinced that it has been wrong in rejecting the pathogenic wish and may be led into accepting it wholly or in part; or the wish itself may be directed to a higher and consequently unobjectionable aim (this is what we call its 'sublimation'); or the rejection of the wish may be recognized as a justifiable one, but the automatic and therefore inefficient mechanism of repression may be replaced by a condemning judgement with the help of the highest human mental functions – conscious control of the wish is attained.

You must forgive me if I have not succeeded in giving you a more clearly intelligible account of these basic positions adopted by the method of treatment that is now described as 'psycho-analysis'. The difficulties have not lain only in the novelty of the subject. The nature of the incompatible wishes which, in spite of repression, succeed in making their existence in the unconscious perceptible, and the subjective and constitutional determinants which must be present in anyone before a failure of repression can occur and a substitute or symptom to be formed – on all this I shall have more light to throw in some of my later remarks.

THIRD LECTURE

LADIES AND GENTLEMEN, It is not always easy to tell the truth, especially when one has to be concise; and I am thus today obliged to correct a wrong statement that I made in my last lecture. I said to you that, having dispensed with hypnosis, I insisted on my patients nevertheless telling me what occurred to them in connexion with the subject under discussion, and assured them that they really knew everything that they had ostensibly forgotten and that the idea that occurred to them* would infallibly contain what we were in search of; and I went on to say to you that I found that the first idea occurring to my patients did in fact produce the right thing and turned out to be the forgotten continuation of the memory. This, however, is not in general the case, and I only put the matter so simply for the sake of brevity. Actually it was only for the first few times that the right thing which had been forgotten turned up as a result of simple insistence on my part. When the procedure was carried further, ideas kept on emerging that could not be the right ones, since they were not appropriate and were rejected as being wrong by the patients themselves. Insistence was of no further help at this point, and I found myself once more regretting my abandonment of hypnosis.

While I was thus at a loss, I clung to a prejudice the scientific justification for which was proved years later by my friend C. G. Jung and his pupils in Zürich. I am bound to

*[The German word here is *Einfall*, which is often translated 'association'; but the latter is a question-begging word, since the whole point at issue is whether what occurs to the patient is in fact an association or not. It is therefore avoided here as far as possible, even at the price of such long paraphrases as the present one. When, however, we come to '*freier Einfall*', 'free association' (though still objectionable) is hardly to be escaped.]

say that it is sometimes most useful to have prejudices. I cherished a high opinion of the strictness with which mental processes are determined, and I found it impossible to believe that an idea produced by a patient while his attention was on the stretch could be an arbitrary one and unrelated to the idea we were in search of. The fact that the two ideas were not identical could be satisfactorily explained from the postulated psychological state of affairs. In the patient under treatment two forces were in operation against each other: on the one hand, his conscious endeavour to bring into consciousness the forgotten idea in his unconscious, and on the other hand, the resistance we already know about, which was striving to prevent what was repressed or its derivatives from thus becoming conscious. If this resistance amounted to little or nothing, what had been forgotten became conscious without distortion. It was accordingly plausible to suppose that the greater the resistance against what we were in search of becoming conscious, the greater would be its distortion. The idea which occurred to the patient in place of what we were in search of had thus itself originated like a symptom: it was a new, artificial, and ephemeral substitute for what had been repressed, and was dissimilar to it in proportion to the degree of distortion it had undergone under the influence of the resistance. But, owing to its nature as a symptom, it must nevertheless have a certain similarity to what we were in search of; and if the resistance were not too great, we ought to be able to guess the latter from the former. The idea occurring to the patient must be in the nature of an *allusion* to the repressed element, like a representation of it in indirect speech.

We know cases in the field of normal mental life in which situations analogous to the one we have just assumed produce similar results. One such case is that of jokes. The problems of psycho-analytic technique have compelled me to investigate the technique of making jokes. I will give you

one example of this – incidentally, a joke in English.
This is the anecdote.* Two not particularly scrupulous
business men had succeeded, by dint of a series of highly
risky enterprises, in amassing a large fortune, and they were
now making efforts to push their way into good society.
One method, which struck them as a likely one, was to have
their portraits painted by the most celebrated and highly-
paid artist in the city, whose pictures had an immense reputation. The precious canvases were shown for the first time
at a large evening party, and the two hosts themselves led
the most influential connoisseur and art critic up to the wall
on which the portraits were hanging side by side, in order
to extract his admiring judgement on them. He studied the
works for a long time, and then, shaking his head, as though
there was something he had missed, pointed to the gap between the pictures and asked quietly: 'But where's the
Saviour?' I see you are all much amused at this joke. Let us
now proceed to examine it. Clearly what the connoisseur
meant to say was: 'You are a couple of rogues, like the
two thieves between whom the Saviour was crucified.' But
he did not say this. Instead he made a remark which seems
at first sight strangely inappropriate and irrelevant, but
which we recognize a moment later as an *allusion* to the
insult that he had in mind and as a perfect substitute for
it. We cannot expect to find in jokes *all* the characteristics
that we have attributed to the ideas occurring to our
patients, but we must stress the identity of the *motive* for
the joke and for the idea. Why did the critic not tell the
rogues straight out what he wanted to say? Because he
had excellent counter-motives working against his desire
to say it to their faces. There are risks attendant upon insulting people who are one's hosts and who have at their command the fists of a large domestic staff. One might easily

*Cf. *Jokes and their Relation to the Unconscious*, 1905 [Chapter 11,
Section 11, where the story is discussed at greater length and, incidentally, described as an American one].

meet the fate which I suggested in my last lecture as an analogy for repression. That was the reason why the critic did not express the insult he had in mind directly but in the form of an 'allusion accompanied by omission';* and the same state of things is responsible for our patients' producing a more or less distorted *substitute* instead of the forgotten idea we are in search of.

It is highly convenient, Ladies and Gentlemen, to follow the Zürich school (Bleuler, Jung, etc.) in describing a group of interdependent ideational elements cathected [charged] with affect as a 'complex'. We see, then, that if in our search for a repressed complex in one of our patients we start out from the last thing he remembers, we shall have every prospect of discovering the complex, provided that the patient puts a sufficient number of his free associations at our disposal. Accordingly, we allow the patient to say whatever he likes, and hold fast to the postulate that nothing can occur to him which is not in an indirect fashion dependent on the complex we are in search of. If this method of discovering what is repressed strikes you as unduly circumstantial, I can at least assure you that it is the only practicable one.

When we come to putting this procedure into effect, we are subject to yet another interference. For the patient will often pause and come to a stop, and assert that he can think of nothing to say, and that nothing whatever occurs to his mind. If this were so and if the patient were right, then our procedure would once again have proved ineffective. But closer observation shows that such a stoppage of the flow of ideas never in fact occurs. It *appears* to happen only because the patient holds back or gets rid of the idea that he has become aware of, under the influence of the resistances which disguise themselves as various critical

*[This is one of the particular techniques described in the passage in Freud's book on jokes where the present anecdote occurs.]

judgements about the value of the idea that has occurred to him. We can protect ourselves against this by warning him beforehand of this behaviour and requiring him to take no notice of such criticisms. He must, we tell him, entirely renounce any critical selection of this kind and say whatever comes into his head, even if he considers it incorrect or irrelevant or nonsensical, and above all if he finds it disagreeable to let himself think about what has occurred to him. So long as this ordinance is carried out we are certain of obtaining the material which will put us on the track of the repressed complexes.

This associative material, which the patient contemptuously rejects when he is under the influence of the resistance instead of under the doctor's, serves the psycho-analyst, as it were, as ore from which, with the help of some simple interpretative devices, he extracts its contents of precious metal. If you are anxious to gain a rapid and provisional knowledge of a patient's repressed complexes, without as yet entering into their arrangement and interconnexion, you will employ as a method of examination the 'association experiment' as it has been developed by Jung (1906) and his pupils. This procedure offers the psycho-analyst what qualitative analysis offers the chemist. In the treatment of neurotic patients it can be dispensed with; but it is indispensable for the objective demonstration of complexes and in the examination of the psychoses, which has been embarked on with so much success by the Zürich school.

Working over the ideas that occur to patients when they submit to the main rule of psycho-analysis is not our only technical method of discovering the unconscious. The same purpose is served by two other procedures: the interpretation of patients' dreams and the exploitation of their faulty and haphazard actions.

I must admit, Ladies and Gentlemen, that I hesitated for

a long time whether, instead of giving you this condensed general survey of the whole field of psycho-analysis, it might not be better to present you with a detailed account of dream-interpretation.* I was held back by a purely subjective and seemingly secondary motive. It seemed to me almost indecent in a country which is devoted to practical aims to make my appearance as a 'dream-interpreter', before you could possibly know the importance that can attach to that antiquated and derided art. The interpretation of dreams is in fact the royal road to a knowledge of the unconscious; it is the securest foundation of psycho-analysis and the field in which every worker must acquire his convictions and seek his training. If I am asked how one can become a psycho-analyst, I reply : 'By studying one's own dreams.' Every opponent of psycho-analysis hitherto has, with a nice discrimination, either evaded any consideration of *The Interpretation of Dreams*, or has sought to skirt over it with the most superficial objections. If, on the contrary you can accept the solutions of the problems of dream-life, the novelties with which psycho-analysis confronts your minds will offer you no further difficulties.

You should bear in mind that the dreams which we produce at night have, on the one hand, the greatest external similarity and internal kinship with the creations of insanity, and are, on the other hand, compatible with complete health in waking life. There is nothing paradoxical in the assertion that no one who regards these 'normal' illusions, delusions, and character-changes with astonishment instead of comprehension has the slightest prospect of understanding the abnormal structures of pathological mental states otherwise than as a layman. You may comfortably count almost all psychiatrists among such laymen.

I invite you now to follow me on a brief excursion through the region of dream-problems. When we are awake we are in the habit of treating dreams with the same con-

* *The Interpretation of Dreams*, 1900.

tempt with which patients regard the associations that are demanded of them by the psycho-analyst. We dismiss them, too, by forgetting them as a rule, quickly and completely. Our low opinion of them is based on the strange character even of those dreams that are not confused and meaningless, and on the obvious absurdity and nonsensicalness of other dreams. Our dismissal of them is related to the uninhibited shamelessness and immorality of the tendencies openly exhibited in some dreams. It is well-known that the ancient world did not share this low opinion of dreams. Nor are the lower strata of our own society today in any doubt about the value of dreams; like the peoples of antiquity, they expect them to reveal the future. I confess that I feel no necessity for making any mystical assumptions in order to fill the gaps in our present knowledge, and accordingly I have never been able to find anything to confirm the prophetic nature of dreams. There are plenty of other things – sufficiently wonderful too – to be said about them.

In the first place, not all dreams are alien to the dreamer, incomprehensible and confused. If you inspect the dreams of very young children, from eighteen months upwards, you will find them perfectly simple and easy to explain. Small children always dream of the fulfilment of wishes that were aroused in them the day before but not satisfied. You will need no interpretative art in order to find this simple solution; all you need do is to inquire into the child's experiences on the previous day (the 'dream-day'). Certainly the most satisfactory solution of the riddle of dreams would be to find that adults' dreams too were like those of children – fulfilments of wishful impulses that had come to them on the dream-day. And such in fact is the case. The difficulties in the way of this solution can be overcome step by step if dreams are analysed more closely.

The first and most serious objection is that the content of adults' dreams is as a rule unintelligible and could not look more unlike the fulfilment of a wish. And here is the answer. Such dreams have been subjected to distortion; the psychical process underlying them might originally have been expressed in words quite differently. You must distinguish the *manifest content of the dream*, as you vaguely recollect it in the morning and laboriously (and, as it seems, arbitrarily) clothe it in words, and the *latent dream-thoughts*, which you must suppose were present in the unconscious. This distortion in dreams is the same process that you have already come to know in investigating the formation of hysterical symptoms. It indicates, too, that the same interplay of mental forces is at work in the formation of dreams as in that of symptoms. The manifest content of the dream is the distorted substitute for the unconscious dream-thoughts and this distortion is the work of the ego's forces of defence – of resistances. In waking life these resistances altogether prevent the repressed wishes of the unconscious from entering consciousness; and during the lowered state of sleep they are at least strong enough to oblige them to adopt a veil of disguise. Thereafter, the dreamer can no more understand the meaning of his dreams than the hysteric can understand the connexion and significance of his symptoms.

You can convince yourself that there are such things as latent dream-thoughts and that the relation between them and the manifest content of the dream is really as I have described it, if you carry out an analysis of dreams, the technique of which is the same as that of psycho-analysis. You entirely disregard the apparent connexions between the elements in the manifest dream and collect the ideas that occur to you in connexion with each separate element of the dream by free association according to the psychoanalytic rule of procedure. From this material you arrive at the latent dream-thoughts, just as you arrived at the patient's hidden complexes from his associations to his symptoms and memories. The latent dream-thoughts which have been reached in this way will at once show you how completely justified we have been in tracing back adults' dreams to children's dreams. The true meaning of the dream, which has now taken the place of its manifest content, is always clearly intelligible; it has its starting-point in experiences of the previous day, and proves to be a fulfilment of unsatisfied wishes. The manifest dream, which you know from memory when you wake up, can therefore only be described as a *disguised* fulfilment of *repressed* wishes.

You can also obtain a view, by a kind of synthetic work, of the process which has brought about the distortion of the unconscious dream-thoughts into the manifest content of the dream. We call this process the 'dream-work'. It deserves our closest theoretical interest, since we are able to study in it, as nowhere else, what unsuspected psychical processes can occur in the unconscious, or rather, to put it more accurately, *between* two separate psychical systems like the conscious and unconscious. Among these freshly discovered psychical processes those of *condensation* and *displacement* are especially noticeable. The dream-work is a special case of the effects produced by two different mental groupings on each other – that is, of the consequences of mental splitting; and it seems identical in all essentials with the process of distortion which transforms the repressed complexes into symptoms where there is unsuccessful repression.

You will also learn with astonishment from the analysis of dreams (and most convincingly from that of your own) what an unsuspectedly great part is played in human developments by impressions and experiences of early childhood. In dream-life the child that is in man pursues its existence, as it were, and retains all its characteristics and wishful impulses, even such as have become unserviceable in later life. There will be brought home to you with irresistible force the many developments, repressions, sublimations, and reaction-formations, by means of which a child with a quite other innate endowment grows into what we call a normal man, the bearer, and in part the victim, of the civilization that has been so painfully acquired.

I should like you to notice, too, that the analysis of dreams has shown us that the unconscious makes use of a particular symbolism, especially for representing sexual complexes. This symbolism varies partly from individual to individual; but partly it is laid down in a typical form and seems to coincide with the symbolism which, as we suspect, underlies our myths and fairy tales. It seems not impossible that these creations of the popular mind might find an explanation through the help of dreams.

Lastly, I must warn you not to let yourselves be put out by the objection that the occurrence of anxiety-dreams contradicts our view of dreams as the fulfilments of wishes. Apart from the fact that these anxiety-dreams, like the rest, require interpretation before any judgement can be formed on them, it must be stated quite generally that the anxiety does not depend on the content of the dream in such a simple manner as one might imagine without having more knowledge and taking more account of the determinants of neurotic anxiety. Anxiety is one of the ego's reactions in repudiation of repressed wishes that have become powerful; and its occurrence in dreams as well is very easily explicable when the formation of the dream has been carried out with too much of an eye to the fulfilment of these repressed wishes.

As you see, research into dreams would be justified for its own sake merely by the information it gives us on matters that can with difficulty be discovered in other ways. But we were in fact led to the subject in connexion with the psycho-analytic treatment of neurotics. You will easily understand from what I have already said how it is that dream-interpretation, if it is not made too difficult by the patient's resistances, leads to a knowledge of his hidden and repressed wishes and of the complexes nourished by them; and I can now pass on to the third group of mental phenomena whose study has become one of the technical instruments of psycho-analysis.

The phenomena in question are the small faulty actions performed by both normal and neurotic people, to which as a rule no importance is attached: forgetting things that might be known and sometimes in fact *are* known (e.g. the occasional difficulty in recalling proper names), slips of the tongue in talking, by which we ourselves are so often affected, analogous slips of the pen and misreadings, bungling the performance of actions, losing objects or breaking them. All of these are things for which as a rule no psychological determinants are sought and which are allowed to pass without criticism as consequences of distraction or inattention or similar causes. Besides these there are the actions and gestures which people carry out without noticing them at all, to say nothing of attributing any psychological importance to them: playing about and fiddling with things, humming tunes, fingering parts of one's own body or one's clothing, and so on.* These small things, faulty actions and symptomatic or haphazard actions alike, are not so insignificant as people, by a sort of conspiracy of silence, are ready to suppose. They always have a meaning, which can usually be interpreted with ease and certainty from the situation in which they occur. And it turns out that once again they give expression to impulses and intentions which have to be kept back and hidden from one's own consciousness, or that they are actually derived from the same repressed wishful impulses and complexes which we have already come to know as the creators of symptoms and the constructors of dreams. They therefore deserve to be rated as symptoms, and if they are examined they may lead, just as dreams do, to the uncovering of the hidden part of the mind. A man's most intimate secrets are as a rule betrayed

*Cf. *The Psychopathology of Everyday Life*, 1901.

by their help. If they occur particularly easily and frequently even in healthy people in whom the repression of unconscious impulses has on the whole been quite successful, they have their triviality and inconspicuousness to thank for it. But they can claim a high theoretical value, since they prove that repression and the formation of substitutes occur even under healthy conditions.

As you already see, psycho-analysts are marked by a particularly strict belief in the determination of mental life. For them there is nothing trivial, nothing arbitrary or haphazard. They expect in every case to find sufficient motives where, as a rule, no such expectation is raised. Indeed, they are prepared to find *several* motives for one and the same mental occurrence whereas what seems to be our innate craving for causality declares itself satisfied with a *single* psychical cause.

If you will now bring together the means we possess for uncovering what is concealed, forgotten, and repressed in the mind (the study of the ideas occurring to patients under free association, of their dreams, and of their faulty and symptomatic actions), and if you will add to these the exploitation of certain other phenomena which occur during psycho-analytic treatment and on which I shall have a few remarks to make later under the heading of 'transference' − if you bear all these in mind, you will agree with me in concluding that our technique is already efficient enough to fulfil its task, to bring the pathogenic psychical material into consciousness and so to get rid of the ailments that have been brought about by the formation of substitutive symptoms. And if, in the course of our therapeutic endeavours, we extend and deepen our knowledge of the human mind both in health and sickness, that can, of course, only be regarded as a peculiar attraction in our work.

You may have formed an impression that the technique

through whose armoury I have just conducted you is particularly difficult. In my opinion that technique is entirely in conformity with the material with which it has to deal. But this much at least is clear : it is not a self-evident one and it must be learnt just as the techniques of histology or surgery must be learnt. You will perhaps be surprised to hear that in Europe we have heard a large number of judgements on psycho-analysis from people who know nothing of this technique and do not employ it; and who go on to demand with apparent scorn that we shall prove to them the correctness of our findings. Among these adversaries there are no doubt some to whom a scientific mode of thought is not as a rule alien, who, for instance, would not reject the results of a microscopic examination because it could not be confirmed on the anatomical preparation with the naked eye, but who would first form a judgement on the matter themselves with the help of a microscope. But, where psycho-analysis is concerned, the prospects of recognition are in truth less favourable. Psycho-analysis is seeking to bring to conscious recognition the things in mental life which are repressed; and everyone who forms a judgement on it is himself a human being, who possesses similar repressions and may perhaps be maintaining them with difficulty. They are therefore bound to call up the same resistance in him as in our patients; and that resistance finds it easy to disguise itself as an intellectual rejection and to bring up arguments like those which we ward off in our patients by means of the fundamental rule of psycho-analysis. We often become aware in our opponents, just as we do in our patients, that their power of judgement is very noticeably influenced affectively in the sense of being diminished. The arrogance of consciousness (in rejecting dreams with such contempt, for instance) is one of the most powerful of the devices with which we are provided as a universal protection against the incursion of unconscious complexes. That is why it is so hard to convince people of the reality of the unconscious and to teach them to recognize something new which is in contradiction to their conscious knowledge.

FOURTH LECTURE

LADIES AND GENTLEMEN, You will want to know now what we have found out about the pathogenic complexes and repressed wishful impulses of neurotics with the help of the technical methods I have described.

First and foremost we have found out one thing. Psychoanalytic research traces back the symptoms of patients' illnesses with really surprising regularity to impressions from their *erotic life*. It shows us that the pathogenic wishful impulses are in the nature of erotic instinctual components; and it forces us to suppose that among the influences leading to the illness the predominant significance must be assigned to erotic disturbances, and that this is the case in both sexes.

I am aware that this assertion of mine will not be willingly believed. Even workers who are ready to follow my psychological studies are inclined to think that I over-estimate the part played by sexual factors; they meet me with the question why *other* mental excitations should not lead to the phenomena I have described of repression and the formation of substitutes. I can only answer that I do not know why they should not, and that I should have no objection to their doing so; but experience shows that they do not carry this weight, that at most they *support* the operation of the sexual factors but cannot replace them. Far from this position having been postulated by me theoretically, at the time of the joint publication of the *Studies* with Dr Breuer in 1895 I had not yet adopted it; and I was only converted to it when my experiences became more numerous and penetrated into the subject more deeply. There are among my present audience a few of my closest friends and followers, who have travelled with me here to Worcester.

Inquire from them, and you will hear that they all began by completely disbelieving my assertion that sexual aetiology was of decisive importance, until their own analytic experiences compelled them to accept it.

A conviction of the correctness of this thesis was not precisely made easier by the behaviour of patients. Instead of willingly presenting us with information about their sexual life, they try to conceal it by every means in their power. People are in general not candid over sexual matters. They do not show their sexuality freely, but to conceal it they wear a heavy overcoat woven of a tissue of lies, as though the weather were bad in the world of sexuality. Nor are they mistaken. It is a fact that sun and wind are not favourable to sexual activity in this civilized world of ours; none of us can reveal his erotism freely to others. But when your patients discover that they can feel quite easy about it while they are under your treatment, they discard this veil of lies, and only then are you in a position to form a judgement on this debatable question. Unluckily even doctors are not preferred above other human creatures in their personal relation to questions of sexual life, and many of them are under the spell of the combination of prudery and prurience which governs the attitude of most 'civilized people' in matters of sexuality.

Let me now proceed with my account of our findings. In another set of cases psycho-analytic investigation traces the symptoms back, it is true, not to sexual experiences but to commonplace traumatic ones. But this distinction loses its significance owing to another circumstance. For the work of analysis required for the thorough explanation and complete recovery of a case never comes to a stop at events that occurred at the time of the onset of the illness, but invariably goes back to the patient's puberty and early childhood; and it is only there that it comes upon the impressions and events which determined the later onset of the illness. It is only experiences in childhood that explain susceptibility to later traumas and it is only by uncovering these almost invariably forgotten memory-traces and by making them conscious that we acquire the power to get rid of the symptoms. And here we reach the same conclusion as in our investigation of dreams: the imperishable, repressed, wishful impulses of childhood have alone provided the power for the construction of symptoms, and without them the reaction to later traumas would have taken a normal course. But these powerful wishful impulses of childhood may without exception be described as sexual.

And now at last I am quite certain that I have surprised you. 'Is there such a thing, then, as infantile sexuality?' you will ask. 'Is not childhood on the contrary the period of life that is marked by the absence of the sexual instinct?' No, Gentlemen, it is certainly not the case that the sexual instinct enters into children at the age of puberty in the way in which, in the Gospel, the devil entered into the swine. A child has its sexual instincts and activities from the first; it comes into the world with them; and, after an important course of development passing through many stages, they lead to what is known as the normal sexuality of the adult. There is even no difficulty in observing the manifestations of these sexual activities in children; on the contrary, it calls for some skill to overlook them or explain them away.

By a lucky chance I am in a position to call a witness in favour of my assertions from your very midst. I have here in my hand a paper written by a Dr Sanford Bell, which was published in *The American Journal of Psychology* in 1902. The author is a Fellow of Clark University, of the very institution in whose lecture-room we are now assembled. In this work, which is entitled 'A Preliminary Study of the Emotion of Love between the Sexes', and which appeared three years before my *Three Essays on the Theory of Sexuality* [1905], the author says exactly what I have just told you: 'The emotion of sex-love ... does not make its appearance for the first time at the period of adolescence, as has been thought.' He carried out his work in what we in Europe would call 'the American manner', collecting no fewei than 2,500 positive observations in the course of fifteen years, among them 800 of his own. Concerning the signs by which these instances of falling in love are revealed he writes as follows: 'The unprejudiced mind in observing these manifestations in hundreds of couples of children cannot escape referring them to sex origin. The most exacting mind is satisfied when to these observations are added the confessions of those who have, as children, experienced the emotion to a marked degree of intensity and whose memories of childhood are relatively distinct.' But those of you who do not wish to believe in infantile sexuality will be most of all surprised to hear that not a few of these children who have fallen in love so early are of the tender age of three, four, and five.

It would not astonish me if you were to attach more credence to these observations made by one of your closest neighbours than to mine. I myself have recently been fortunate enough to obtain a fairly complete picture of the somatic instinctual manifestations and mental products at an early stage of a child's erotic life from the analysis of a five-year-old boy, suffering from anxiety – an analysis carried out with a correct technique by his own father.* And I may remind you that only a few hours ago, in this same room, my friend Dr C. G. Jung reported an observation to you made on a still younger girl who, with a precipitating cause similar to my patient's (the birth of a younger child in the family), made it possible to infer with certainty the presence of almost the same sensual impulses, wishes, and complexes. [Cf. Jung, 1910.] I do not despair, therefore, of your becoming reconciled to what seems at first sight the strange idea of infantile sexuality. And I should like to

* 'The Analysis of a Phobia in a Five-Year-Old Boy' [1909].

quote to you the praiseworthy example of the Zürich psychiatrist, Dr E. Bleuler, who declared publicly not many years ago that he was 'unable to comprehend my theories of sexuality', and who has since then confirmed the existence of infantile sexuality to its full extent from his own observations. (Cf. Bleuler, 1908.)

It is only too easy to explain why most people (whether medical observers or others) will hear nothing of the sexual life of children. They have forgotten their own infantile sexual activity under the pressure of their education to a civilized life, and they do not wish to be reminded of what has been repressed. They would arrive at other convictions if they were to begin their inquiry with a self-analysis, a revision and interpretation of their childhood memories.

Put away your doubts, then, and join me in a consideration of infantile sexuality from the earliest age.* A child's sexual instinct turns out to be put together out of a number of factors; it is capable of being divided up into numerous components which originate from various sources. Above all, it is still independent of the reproductive function, into the service of which it will later be brought. It serves for the acquisition of different kinds of pleasurable feeling, which, basing ourselves on analogies and connexions, we bring together under the idea of sexual pleasure. The chief source of infantile sexual pleasure is the appropriate excitation of certain parts of the body that are especially susceptible to stimulus: apart from the genitals, these are the oral, anal, and urethral orifices, as well as the skin and other sensory surfaces. Since at this first phase of infantile sexual life satisfaction is obtained from the subject's own body and extraneous objects are disregarded, we term this phase (from a word coined by Havelock Ellis) that of *auto-erotism*. We call the parts of the body that are important in the acquisition of sexual pleasure 'erotogenic zones'.

*Cf. *Three Essays on the Theory of Sexuality*, 1905.

Thumb-sucking (or sensual sucking) in the youngest infants is a good example of this auto-erotic satisfaction from an erotogenic zone. The first scientific observer of this phenomenon, a paediatrician in Budapest named Lindner (1879), already interpreted it correctly as sexual satisfaction and described exhaustively its transition to other and higher forms of sexual activity. Another sexual satisfaction at this period of life is the masturbatory excitation of the genitals, which retains so much importance in later life and by many people is never completely conquered. Alongside these and other auto-erotic activities, we find in children at a very early age manifestations of those instinctual components of sexual pleasure (or, as we like to say, of libido) which presuppose the taking of an extraneous person as an object. These instincts occur in pairs of opposites, active and passive. I may mention as the most important representatives of this group the desire to cause pain (sadism) with its passive counterpart (masochism) and the active and passive desire for looking, from the former of which curiosity branches off later on and from the latter the impulsion to artistic and theatrical display. Others of a child's sexual activities already imply the making of an 'object-choice', where an extraneous person becomes the main feature, a person who owes his importance in the first instance to considerations arising from the self-preservative instinct. But at this early period of childhood difference in sex plays no decisive part as yet. Thus you can attribute some degree of homosexuality to every child without doing him an injustice. This widespread and copious but dissociated sexual life of children, in which each separate instinct pursues its own acquisition of pleasure independently of all the rest, is now brought together and organized in two main directions, so that by the end of puberty the individual's final sexual character is as a rule completely formed. On the one hand, the separate instincts become subordinated to the dominance of the genital zone, so that the whole sexual life enters the service of reproduction, and the satisfaction of the separate instincts retains its importance only as preparing for and encouraging the sexual act proper. On the other hand, object-choice pushes auto-erotism into the background, so that in the subject's erotic life all the components of the sexual instinct now seek satisfaction in relation to the person who is loved. Not all of the original sexual components, however, are admitted to take part in this final establishment of sexuality. Even before puberty extremely energetic repressions of certain instincts have been effected under the influence of education, and mental forces such as shame, disgust, and morality have been set up, which, like watchmen, maintain these repressions. So that when at puberty the high tide of sexual demands is reached, it is met by these mental reactive or resistant structures like dams, which direct its flow into what are called normal channels and make it impossible for it to reactivate the instincts that have undergone repression. It is in particular the coprophilic impulses of childhood – that is to say, the desires attaching to the excreta – which are submitted the most rigorously to repression, and the same is true, furthermore, of fixation to the figures to which the child's original object-choice was attached.

There is a dictum in general pathology, Gentlemen, which asserts that every developmental process carries with it the seed of a pathological disposition, in so far as that process may be inhibited, delayed, or may run its course incompletely. The same thing is true of the highly complicated development of the sexual function. It does not occur smoothly in every individual; and, if not, it leaves behind it either abnormalities or a predisposition to fall ill later, along the path of involution (i.e. regression). It may happen that not all the component instincts submit to the dominance of the genital zone. An instinct which remains in this way independent leads to what we describe as a *perversion*, and may substitute its own sexual aim for the normal one. It very often happens, as I have already said, that auto-erotism is not completely conquered, and evidence of this is given by a great variety of subsequent disturbances. The originally equal value attached to the two sexes as sexual objects may persist, and this will lead to a tendency in adult life to homosexual activity, which can in certain circumstances be intensified into exclusive homosexuality. These classes of disturbance represent direct inhibitions in the development of the sexual function; they comprise the perversions and, what is by no means rare, general infantilism in sexual life.

The predisposition to *neurosis* is traceable to impaired sexual development in a different way. Neuroses are related to perversions as negative to positive. The same instinctual components as in the perversions can be observed in the neuroses as vehicles of complexes and constructors of symptoms, but in the latter case they operate from the unconscious. Thus they have undergone repression, but have been able, in defiance of it, to persist in the unconscious. Psychoanalysis makes it clear that an excessively strong manifestation of these instincts at a very early age leads to a kind of partial *fixation*, which then constitutes a weak point in the structure of the sexual function. If in maturity the performance of the normal sexual function comes up against obstacles, the repression that took place during the course of development will be broken through at the precise points at which the infantile fixations occurred.

But here you will perhaps protest that all this is not sexuality. I have been using the word in a far wider sense than that in which you been accustomed to understand it. So much I am quite ready to grant you. But the question arises whether it is not rather you who have been using the word in far too narrow a sense by restricting it to the sphere of reproduction. It means that you are sacrificing an understanding of the perversions and the connexion between the perversions, the neuroses, and normal sexual life; and you are making it impossible for you to recognize in its true significance the easily observable beginnings of the somatic and mental erotic life of children. But however you may choose to decide the verbal usage, you should bear firmly in mind that psycho-analysts understand sexuality in the full sense to which one is led by a consideration of infantile sexuality.

Let us return to the sexual development of children. We have some arrears to make up owing to our having paid more attention to the somatic than to the mental phenomena of sexual life. The child's first choice of an object, which derives from its need for help, claims our further interest. Its choice is directed in the first instance to all those who look after it, but these soon give place to its parents. Children's relations to their parents, as we learn alike from direct observation of children and from later analytic examination of adults, are by no means free from elements of accompanying sexual excitation. The child takes both of its parents, and more particularly one of them, as the object of its erotic wishes. In so doing, it usually follows some indication from its parents, whose affection bears the clearest characteristics of a sexual activity, even though of one that is inhibited in its aims. As a rule a father prefers his daughter and a mother her son; the child reacts to this by wishing, if he is a son, to take his father's place, and, if she is a daughter, her mother's. The feelings which are aroused in these relations between parents and children and in the resulting ones between brothers and sisters are not only of a positive or affectionate kind but also of a negative or hostile one. The complex which is thus formed is doomed to early repression; but it continues to exercise a great and lasting influence from the unconscious. It is to be suspected that, together with its extensions, it constitutes the *nuclear complex* of every neurosis, and we may expect to find it no less actively at work in other regions of mental life. The myth of King Oedipus, who killed his father and took his mother to wife, reveals, with little modification, the infantile wish, which is later opposed and repudiated by the *barrier against incest*. Shakespeare's *Hamlet* is equally rooted in the soil of the incest-complex, but under a better disguise.*

During the time when the child is dominated by the still unrepressed nuclear complex, an important part of his intellectual activity is brought into the service of his sexual interests. He begins to inquire where babies come from, and, on the basis of the evidence presented to him, guesses more of the true facts than the grown-ups imagine. His interest in these researches is usually set going by the very real threat offered to him by the arrival of a new baby, which to begin with he regards merely as a competitor. Under the influence of the component instincts that are active in himself, he arrives at a number of 'infantile sexual theories' – such as attributing a male genital organ to both sexes alike, or supposing that babies are conceived by eating and born through the end of the bowel, or regarding sexual intercourse as a hostile act, a kind of violent subjugation. But as a result precisely of the incompleteness of his sexual constitution, and of the gap in his knowledge due to the hidden nature of the female sexual channel, the young investigator is obliged to abandon his work as a failure. The fact of this childish research itself, as well as the different infantile sexual theories that it brings to light, remain of importance in determining the formation of the child's character and the content of any later neurotic illness.

It is inevitable and perfectly normal that a child should take his parents as the first objects of his love. But his

---

* [Though Freud had been familiar with the concept for more than twenty years before this, he adopted the term 'Oedipus complex' for the first time shortly after these lectures were delivered, in the first of his 'Contributions to the Psychology of Love', 1910.]

libido should not remain fixated to these first objects; later on, it should merely take them as a model, and should make a gradual transition from them on to extraneous people when the time for the final choice of an object arrives. The detachment of the child from his parents is thus a task that cannot be evaded if the young individual's social fitness is not to be endangered. During the time at which repression is making its selection among the component instincts, and later, when there should be a slackening of the parents' influence, which is essentially responsible for the expenditure of energy on these repressions, the task of education meets with great problems, which at the present time are certainly not always dealt with in an understanding and unobjectionable manner.

You must not suppose, Ladies and Gentlemen, that these discussions on sexual life and the psychosexual development of children have led us too far from psycho-analysis and the problem of curing nervous disorders. You can, if you like, regard psycho-analytic treatment as no more than a prolongation of education for the purpose of overcoming the residues of childhood.

FIFTH LECTURE

LADIES AND GENTLEMEN, With the discovery of infantile sexuality and the tracing back of neurotic symptoms to erotic instinctual components we have arrived at some unexpected formulas concerning the nature and purposes of neurotic illnesses. We see that human beings fall ill when, as a result of external obstacles or of an internal lack of adaptation, the satisfaction of their erotic needs *in reality* is frustrated. We see that they then take flight into *illness* in order that by its help they may find a satisfaction to take the place of what has been frustrated. We recognize that the pathological symptoms constitute a portion of the subject's sexual activity or even the whole of his sexual life, and we find that the withdrawal from reality is the main purpose of the illness but also the main damage caused by it. We suspect that our patients' resistance to recovery is no simple one, but compounded of several motives. Not only does the patient's ego rebel against giving up the repressions by means of which it has risen above its original disposition, but the sexual instincts are unwilling to renounce their substitutive satisfaction so long as it is uncertain whether reality will offer them anything better.

The flight from unsatisfactory reality into what, on account of the biological damage involved, we call illness (though it is never without an immediate yield of pleasure to the patient) takes place along the path of involution, of regression, of a return to earlier phases of sexual life, phases from which at one time satisfaction was not withheld. This regression appears to be a twofold one: a *temporal* one, in so far as the libido, the erotic needs, hark back to stages of development that are earlier in time, and a *formal* one, in that the original and primitive methods of psychical expression are employed in manifesting those needs. Both these kinds of regression, however, lead back to childhood and unite in bringing about an infantile condition of sexual life.

The deeper you penetrate into the pathogenesis of nervous illness, the more you will find revealed the connexion between the neuroses and other productions of the human mind, including the most valuable. You will be taught that we humans, with the high standards of our civilization and under the pressure of our internal repressions, find reality unsatisfying quite generally, and for that reason entertain a life of phantasy in which we like to make up for the insufficiencies of reality by the production of wish-fulfilments. These phantasies include a great deal of the true constitutional essence of the subject's personality as well as of those of his impulses which are repressed where reality is concerned. The energetic and successful man is one who succeeds by his efforts in turning his wishful phantasies into reality. Where this fails, as a result of the resistance of the external world and of the subject's own weakness, he begins to turn away from reality and withdraws into his more satisfying world of phantasy, the content of which is transformed into symptoms should he fall ill. In certain favourable circumstances, it still remains possible for him to find another path leading from these phantasies to reality, instead of becoming permanently estranged from it by regressing to infancy. If a person who is at loggerheads with reality possesses an *artistic gift* (a thing that is still a psychological mystery to us), he can transform his phantasies into artistic creations instead of into symptoms. In this manner he can escape the doom of neurosis and by this roundabout path regain his contact with reality. (Cf. Rank, 1907.) If there is persistent rebellion against the real world and if this precious gift is absent or insufficient, it is almost inevitable that the libido, keeping to the sources of the phantasies, will follow the path of regression, and will revive infantile wishes and end in neurosis. Today neurosis takes the place of the monasteries which used to be the refuge of all whom life had disappointed or who felt too weak to face it.

Let me at this point state the principal finding to which we have been led by the psycho-analytic investigation of neurotics. The neuroses have no psychical content that is peculiar to them and that might not equally be found in healthy people. Or, as Jung has expressed it, neurotics fall ill of the same complexes against which we healthy people struggle as well. Whether that struggle ends in health, in neurosis, or in a countervailing superiority of achievement, depends on *quantitative* considerations, on the relative strength of the conflicting forces.

I have not yet told you, Ladies and Gentlemen, of the most important of the observations which confirm our hypothesis of the sexual instinctual forces operating in neuroses. In every psycho-analytic treatment of a neurotic patient the strange phenomenon that is known as 'transference' makes its appearance. The patient, that is to say, directs towards the physician a degree of affectionate feeling (mingled, often enough, with hostility) which is based on no real relation between them and which – as is shown by every detail of its emergence – can only be traced back to old wishful phantasies of the patient's which have become unconscious. Thus the part of the patient's emotional life which he can no longer recall to memory is re-experienced by him in his relation to the physician; and it is only this re-experiencing in the 'transference' that convinces him of the existence and of the power of these unconscious sexual impulses. His symptoms, to take an analogy from chemistry, are precipitates of earlier experiences in the sphere of love (in the widest sense of the word), and it is only in the raised temperature of his experience of the transference that they can be resolved and reduced to other psychical products. In this reaction the physician, if I may borrow an apt phrase from Ferenczi (1909), plays the part of a catalytic ferment, which temporarily attracts to itself the affects liberated in the process. A study of transference, too, can give you the key to an understanding of hypnotic suggestion, which we employed to begin with as a technical method for investigating the unconscious in our patients. At that time hypnosis was found to be a help therapeutically, but a hindrance to the scientific understanding of the facts; for it cleared away the psychical resistances in a certain area while building them up into an unscalable wall at its frontiers. You must not suppose, moreover, that the phenomenon of transference (of which, unfortunately, I can tell you all too little today) is *created* by psycho-analytic influence. Transference arises spontaneously in all human relationships just as it does between the patient and the physician. It is everywhere the true vehicle of therapeutic influence; and the less its presence is suspected, the more powerfully it operates. So psycho-analysis does not create it, but merely reveals it to consciousness and gains control of it in order to guide psychical processes towards the desired goal. I cannot, however, leave the topic of transference without stressing the fact that this phenomenon plays a decisive part in bringing conviction not only to the patient but also to the physician. I know it to be true of all my followers that they were only convinced of the correctness of my assertions on the pathogenesis of the neuroses by their experiences with transference; and I can very well understand that such certainty of judgement cannot be attained before one has carried out psycho-analyses and has oneself observed the workings of transference.

Ladies and Gentlemen, from the intellectual point of view we must, I think, take into account two special obstacles to recognizing psycho-analytic trains of thought. In the first place, people are unaccustomed to reckoning with a strict and universal application of determinism to mental life; and in the second place, they are ignorant of the peculiarities which distinguish unconscious mental processes from the conscious ones that are familiar to us. One of the most widespread resistances to psycho-analytic work, in the sick and healthy alike, can be traced to the second of these two factors. People are afraid of doing harm by psycho-analysis; they are afraid of bringing the repressed sexual instincts into the patient's consciousness, as though that involved a danger of their overwhelming his higher ethical trends and of their robbing him of his cultural acquisitions. People notice that the patient has sore spots in his mind, but shrink from touching them for fear of increasing his sufferings. We can accept this analogy. It is no doubt kinder not to touch diseased spots if it can do nothing else but cause pain. But, as we know, a surgeon does not refrain from examining and handling a focus of disease, if he is intending to take active measures which he believes will lead to a permanent cure. No one thinks of blaming him for the inevitable suffering caused by the examination or for the reactions to the operation, if only it gains its end and the patient achieves a lasting recovery as a result of the temporary worsening of his state. The case is similar with psycho-analysis. It may make the same claims as surgery: the increase in suffering which it causes the patient during treatment is incomparably less than what a surgeon causes, and is quite negligible in proportion to the severity of the underlying ailment. On the other hand, the final outcome that is so much dreaded – the destruction of the patient's cultural character by the instincts which have been set free from repression – is totally impossible. For alarm on this score takes no account of what our experiences have taught us with certainty – namely that the mental and somatic power of a wishful impulse, when once its repression has failed, is far stronger if it is unconscious than if it is conscious; so that to make it conscious can only be to weaken it. An unconscious wish cannot be influenced and it is independent of any contrary tendencies, whereas a conscious one is inhibited by whatever else is conscious and opposed to it. Thus the work of psycho-analysis puts itself at the orders of precisely the highest and most valuable cultural trends, as a better substitute for the unsuccessful repression.

What, then, becomes of the unconscious wishes which have been set free by psycho-analysis? Along what paths do we succeed in making them harmless to the subject's life? There are several such paths. The most frequent outcome is that, while the work is actually going on, these wishes are destroyed by the rational mental activity of the better impulses that are opposed to them. *Repression* is replaced by a *condemning judgement* carried out along the best lines. That is possible because what we have to get rid of is to a great extent only the consequences arising from earlier stages of the ego's development. The subject only succeeded in the past in repressing the unserviceable instinct because he himself was at that time still imperfectly organized and feeble. In his present-day maturity and strength, he will perhaps be able to master what is hostile to him with complete success.

A second outcome of the work of psycho-analysis is that it then becomes possible for the unconscious instincts revealed by it to be employed for the useful purposes which they would have found earlier if development had not been interrupted. For the extirpation of the infantile wishful impulses is by no means the ideal aim of development. Owing to their repressions, neurotics have sacrificed many sources of mental energy whose contributions would have been of great value in the formation of their character and in their activity in life. We know of a far more expedient process of development, called '*sublimation*', in which the energy of the infantile wishful impulses is not cut off but remains ready for use – the unserviceable aim of the various impulses being replaced by one that is higher, and perhaps no longer sexual. It happens to be precisely the components of the *sexual* instinct that are specially marked by a capacity of this kind for sublimation, for exchanging. their sexual aim for another one which is comparatively remote and socially valuable. It is probable that we owe our highest cultural successes to the contribution of energy made in this way to our mental functions. Premature repression makes the sublimation of the repressed instinct impossible; when the repression is lifted, the path to sublimation becomes free once more.

We must not omit to consider the third of the possible outcomes of the work of psycho-analysis. A certain portion of the repressed libidinal impulses has a claim to direct satisfaction and ought to find it in life. Our civilized standards make life too difficult for the majority of human organizations. Those standards consequently encourage the retreat from reality and the generating of neuroses, without achieving any surplus of cultural gain by this excess of sexual repression. We ought not to exalt ourselves so high as completely to neglect what was originally animal in our nature. Nor should we forget that the satisfaction of the individual's happiness cannot be erased from among the aims of our civilization. The plasticity of the components of sexuality, shown by their capacity for sublimation, may indeed offer a great temptation to strive for still greater cultural achievements by still further sublimation. But, just as we do not count on our machines converting more than a certain fraction of the heat consumed into useful mechanical work, we ought not to seek to alienate the whole amount of the energy of the sexual instinct from its proper ends. We cannot succeed in doing so; and if the restriction upon sexuality were to be carried too far it would inevitably bring with it all the evils of soil-exhaustion.

It may be that you for your part will regard the warning with which I close as an exaggeration. I shall only venture on an indirect picture of my conviction by telling you an old story and leaving you to make what use you like of it. German literature is familiar with a little town called Schilda, to whose inhabitants clever tricks of every possible sort are attributed. The citizens of Schilda, so we are told, possessed a horse with whose feats of strength they were highly pleased and against which they had only one objection – that it consumed such a large quantity of expensive oats. They determined to break it of this bad habit very gently by reducing its ration by a few stalks every day, till they had accustomed it to complete abstinence. For a time things went excellently: the horse was weaned to the point of eating only one stalk a day, and on the succeeeding day it was at length to work without any oats at all. On the morning of that day the spiteful animal was found dead; and the citizens of Schilda could not make out what it had died of.

We should be inclined to think that the horse was starved and that no work at all could be expected of an animal without a certain modicum of oats.

I must thank you for your invitation and for the attention with which you have listened to me.

THE QUESTION OF LAY ANALYSIS

Conversations with an Impartial Person
(1926)

INTRODUCTION

THE title of this small work is not immediately intelligible.
I will therefore explain it. 'Layman' = 'Non-doctor'; and
the question is whether non-doctors as well as doctors are
to be allowed to practise analysis. This question has its
limitations both in time and place. In *time*, because up to
now no one has been concerned as to *who* practises analysis.
Indeed, people have been much too little concerned about
it – the one thing they were agreed on was a wish that *no
one* should practise it. Various reasons were given for this,
but they were based on the same underlying distaste. Thus
the demand that only doctors should analyse corresponds
to a new and apparently more friendly attitude to analysis
– if, that is, it can escape the suspicion of being after all
only a slightly modified derivative of the earlier attitude.
It is conceded that in some circumstances an analytic treatment shall be undertaken; but, if so, only doctors are to
undertake it. The reason for this restriction then becomes
a matter for inquiry.

The question is limited in *place* because it does not arise
in all countries with equal significance. In Germany and
America it would be no more than an academic discussion;
for in those countries every patient can have himself treated
how and by whom he chooses, and anyone who chooses
can, as a 'quack', handle any patients, provided only that
he undertakes the responsibility for his actions.* The law
does not intervene until it is called in to expiate some injury
done to the patient. But in Austria, in which and for which
I am writing, there is a preventive law, which forbids non-
doctors from undertaking the treatment of patients, with-

---

*[This is actually true only of *certain* of the United States. It is
also true of Great Britain.]

out waiting for its outcome.* So here the question whether laymen (= non-doctors) may treat patients by psycho-analysis has a practical sense. As soon as it is raised, how-ever, it appears to be settled by the wording of the law. Neurotics are patients, laymen are non-doctors, psycho-analysis is a procedure for curing or improving nervous disorders, and all such treatments are reserved to doctors. It follows that laymen are not permitted to practise analysis on neurotics, **and** are punishable if they nevertheless do so. The position being so simple, one hardly ventures to take up the question of lay analysis. All the same, there are some complications, which the law does not trouble about, but which nevertheless call for consideration. It may perhaps turn out that in this instance the patients are not like other patients, that the laymen are not really laymen, and that the doctors have not exactly the qualities which one has a right to expect of doctors and on which their claims should be based. If this can be proved, there will be justifiable grounds for demanding that the law shall not be applied without modification to the instance before us.

*The same holds good in France

I

WHETHER this happens will depend on people who are not obliged to be familiar with the peculiarities of an analytic treatment. It is our task to give information on the subject to these impartial persons, whom we shall assume to be, at the moment, still in ignorance. It is to be regretted that we cannot let them be present as an audience at a treatment of this kind. But the 'analytic situation' allows the presence of no third person. Moreover the different sessions are of very unequal value. An unauthorized listener who hit upon a chance one of them would as a rule form no useful impression; he would be in danger of not understanding what was passing between the analyst and the patient, or he would be bored. For good or ill, therefore, he must be content with our information, which we shall try to make as trustworthy as possible.

A patient, then, may be suffering from fluctuations in his moods which he cannot control, or from a sense of despondency by which his energy feels paralysed because he thinks he is incapable of doing anything properly, or from a nervous embarrassment among strangers. He may perceive, without understanding the reason for it, that he has difficulties in carrying out his professional work, or indeed any comparatively important decision or any undertaking. He may one day have suffered from a distressing attack – unknown in its origin – of feelings of anxiety, and since then have been unable, without a struggle, to walk along the street alone, or to travel by train; he may perhaps have had to give up both entirely. Or, a very remarkable thing, his thoughts may go their own way and refuse to be directed by his will. They pursue problems that are quite indifferent to him, but from which he cannot get free. Quite ludicrous

tasks, too, are imposed on him, such as counting up the
windows on the fronts of houses. And when he has performed simple actions such as posting a letter or turning
off a gas-jet, he finds himself a moment later doubting
whether he has really done so. This may be no more than
an annoyance and a nuisance. But his state becomes intolerable if he suddenly finds he is unable to fend off the idea
that he has pushed a child under the wheels of a car or has
thrown a stranger off the bridge into the water, or if he has
to ask himself whether he is not the murderer whom the
police are looking for in connexion with a crime that was
discovered that day. It is obvious nonsense, as he himself
knows; he has never done any harm to anyone; but if he
were really the murderer who is being looked for, his feeling – his sense of guilt – could not be stronger.

Or again our patient – and this time let us make her a
woman – may suffer in another way and in a different field.
She is a pianist, but her fingers are overcome by cramp and
refuse to serve her. Or when she thinks of going to a party
she promptly becomes aware of a call of nature the satisfaction of which would be incompatible with a social
gathering. She has therefore given up going to parties,
dances, theatres, or concerts. She is overcome by violent
headaches or other painful sensations at times when they
are most inconvenient. She may even be unable to keep
down any meal she eats – which can become dangerous in
the long run. And, finally, it is a lamentable fact that she
cannot tolerate any agitations, which after all are inevitable in life. On such occasions she falls in a faint, often
accompanied by muscular spasms that recall sinister pathological states.

Other patients, again, suffer from disturbances in a
particular field in which emotional life converges with demands of a bodily sort. If they are men, they find they are
incapable of giving physical expression to their tenderest
feelings towards the opposite sex, while towards less-loved

objects they may perhaps have every reaction at their command. Or their sensual feelings attach them to people whom they despise and from whom they would like to get free; or those same feelings impose requirements on them whose fulfilment they themselves find repulsive. If they are women, they feel prevented by anxiety or disgust or by unknown obstructions from meeting the demands of sexual life; or, if they have surrendered to love, they find themselves cheated of the enjoyment which nature has provided as a reward for such compliance.

All these people recognize that they are ill and go to doctors, by whom people expect nervous disorders like these to be removed. The doctors, too, lay down the categories into which these complaints are divided. They diagnose them, each according to his own standpoint, under different names: neurasthenia, psychasthenia, phobias, obsessional neurosis, hysteria. They examine the organs which produce the symptoms, the heart, the stomach, the bowels, the genitals, and find them healthy. They recommend interruptions in the patient's accustomed mode of life, holidays, strengthening exercises, tonics, and by these means bring about temporary improvements – or no result at all. Eventually the patients hear that there are people who are concerned quite specially with the treatment of such complaints and start an analysis with them.

During this disquisition on the symptoms of neurotics, the Impartial Person, whom I imagine as being present, has been showing signs of impatience. At this point, however, he becomes attentive and interested. 'So now', he says, 'we shall learn what the analyst does with the patient whom the doctor has not been able to help.'

Nothing takes place between them except that they talk to each other. The analyst makes use of no instruments – not even for examining the patient – nor does he prescribe any medicines. If it is at all possible, he even leaves the patient in his environment and in his usual mode of life during the treatment. This is not a necessary condition of course, and may not always be practicable. The analyst agrees upon a fixed regular hour with the patient, gets him to talk, listens to him, talks to him in his turn, and gets him to listen.

The Impartial Person's features now show signs of unmistakable relief and relaxation, but they also clearly betray some contempt. It is as though he were thinking: 'Nothing more than that? Words, words, words, as Prince Hamlet says.' And no doubt he is thinking too of Mephistopheles' mocking speech* on how comfortably one can get along with the help of words – lines that no German will ever forget.

'So it is a kind of magic,' he comments: 'you talk, and blow away his ailments.'

Quite true. It *would* be magic if it worked rather quicker. An essential attribute of a magician is speed – one might say suddenness – of success. But analytic treatments take months and even years: magic that is so slow loses its miraculous character. And incidently do not let us despise the *word*. After all it is a powerful instrument; it is the means by which we convey our feelings to one another, our method of influencing other people. Words can do unspeakable good and cause terrible wounds. No doubt 'in the beginning was the deed' and the word came later, in some circumstances it meant an advance in civilization when deeds were softened into words. But originally the word was magic – a magical act; and it has retained much of its ancient power.

The Impartial Person proceeds: 'Let us suppose that the patient is no better prepared to understand analytic treatment than I am; then how are you going to make him believe in the magic of the word or of the speech that is to free him from his sufferings?'

Some preparation must of course be given   him; and

* [In his conversation with the student in *Faust*, Part 1, Scene 4.]
† [*Faust*, Part 1, Scene 3.]

there is a simple way of doing it. We call on him to be completely straightforward with his analyst, to keep nothing back intentionally that comes into his head, and then to put aside *every* reservation that might prevent his reporting certain thoughts or memories. Everyone is aware that there are some things in himself that he would be very unwilling to tell other people or that he considers it altogether out of the question to tell. These are his 'intimacies'. He has a notion too – and this represents a great advance in psychological self-knowledge – that there are other things that one would not care to admit *to oneself* : things that one likes to conceal from oneself and which for that reason one breaks off short and drives out of one's thoughts if, in spite of everything, they turn up. Perhaps he may himself notice that a very remarkable psychological problem begins to appear in this situation – of a thought of his own being kept secret from his own self. It looks as though his own self were no longer the unity which he had always considered it to be, as though there were something else as well in him that could confront that self. He may become obscurely aware of a contrast between a self and a mental life in the wider sense. If now he accepts the demand made by analysis that he shall say everything, he will easily become accessible to an expectation that to have relations and exchanges of thought with someone under such unusual conditions might also lead to peculiar results.

'I understand,' says our Impartial Person. 'You assume that every neurotic has something oppressing him, some secret. And by getting him to tell you about it you relieve his oppression and do him good. That, of course, is the principle of Confession, which the Catholic Church has used from time immemorial in order to make secure its dominance over people's minds.'

We must reply: 'Yes and no !' Confession no doubt plays a part in analysis – as an introduction to it, we might say. But it is very far from constituting the essence of analysis or

from explaining its effects. In Confession the sinner tells
what he knows; in analysis the neurotic has to tell more.
Nor have we heard that Confession has ever developed
enough power to get rid of actual pathological symptoms.

'Then, after all, I do not understand,' comes the rejoinder.
'What can you possibly mean by "telling more than he
knows"? But I can well believe that as an analyst you
gain a stronger influence over your patients than a Father
Confessor over his penitents, since your contacts with him
are so much longer, more intensive, and also more individual, and since you use this increased influence to divert him
from his sick thoughts, to talk him out of his fears, and so
on. It would certainly be strange if it were possible by such
means to control purely physical phenomena as well, such
as vomiting, diarrhoea, convulsions; but I know that influence like that is in fact quite possible if a person is put into
a state of hypnosis. By the trouble you take with the patient
you probably succeed in bringing about a hypnotic relation
of that sort with him – a suggestive attachment to yourself
– even though you may not intend to; and in that case the
miraculous results of your treatment are the effect of hypnotic suggestion. But, so far as I know, hypnotic treatment
works much faster than your analysis, which, as you tell
me, lasts for months and years.'

Our Impartial Person cannot be either so ignorant or so
perplexed as we thought to begin with. There are unmistakable signs that he is trying to understand psycho-analysis
with the help of his previous knowledge, that he is trying to
link it up with something he already knows. The difficult
task now lies ahead of us of making it clear to him that he
will not succeed in this: that analysis is a procedure *sui
generis*, something novel and special, which can only be
understood with the help of *new* insights – or hypotheses, if
that sounds better. But he is still waiting for our answer to
his last remarks.

What you say about the special personal influence of the

analyst certainly deserves great attention. An influence of the kind exists and plays a large part in analysis – but not the same part as in hypnotism. It ought to be possible to convince you that the situations in the two cases are quite different. It may be enough to point out that we do not use this personal influence, the factor of 'suggestion', to suppress the symptoms of the illness, as happens with *hypnotic* suggestion. Further, it would be a mistake to believe that this factor is the vehicle and promoter of the treatment throughout its length. At its beginning, no doubt. But later on it opposes our analytic intentions and forces us to adopt the most far-reaching counter-measures. And I should like to show by an example how far diverting a patient's thoughts and talking him out of things are from the technique of analysis. If a patient of ours is suffering from a sense of guilt, as though he had committed a serious crime, we do not recommend him to disregard his qualms of conscience and do not emphasize his undoubted innocence; he himself has often tried to do so without success. What we do is to remind him that such a strong and persistent feeling must after all be based on something real, which it may perhaps be possible to discover.

'It would surprise me', comments the Impartial Person, 'if you were able to soothe your patients by agreeing with their sense of guilt in that way. But what *are* your analytic intentions? and what *do* you do with your patients?'

II

IF I am to say anything intelligible to you, I shall no doubt
have to tell you something of a psychological theory which
is not known or not appreciated outside analytic circles. It
will be easy to deduce from this theory what we want from
our patients and how we obtain it. I shall expound it to you
dogmatically, as though it were a complete theoretical
structure. But do not suppose that it came into being as
such a structure, like a philosophical system. We have developed it very slowly, we have wrestled over every small
detail of it, we have unceasingly modified it, keeping a
continuous contact with observation, till it has finally taken
a shape in which it seems to suffice for our purposes. Only a
few years ago I should have had to clothe this theory in
other terms. Nor, of course, can I guarantee to you that the
form in which it is expressed today will remain the final
one. Science, as you know, is not a revelation; long after its
beginnings it still lacks the attributes of definiteness, immut-
ability, and infallibility for which human thought so deeply
longs. But such as it is, it is all that we can have. If you will
further bear in mind that our science is very young, scarcely
as old as the century, and that it is concerned with what is
perhaps the most difficult material that can be the subject
of human research, you will easily be able to adopt the
correct attitude towards my exposition. But interrupt me
whenever you feel inclined, if you cannot follow me or if
you want further explanations.

'I will interrupt you before you have even begun. You
say that you intend to expound a new psychology to me;
but I should have thought that psychology was no new
science. There have been psychologies and psychologists

enough; and I heard of great achievements in that field while I was at college.'

I should not dream of disputing them. But if you look into the matter more closely you will have to class these great achievements as belonging rather to the physiology of the sense organs. The theory of mental life could not be developed, because it was inhibited by a single essential misunderstanding. What does it comprise today, as it is taught at college? Apart from those valuable discoveries in the physiology of the senses, a number of classifications and definitions of our mental processes which, thanks to linguistic usage, have become the common property of every educated person. That is clearly not enough to give a view of our mental life. Have you not noticed that every philosopher, every imaginative writer, every historian, and every biographer makes up his own psychology for himself, brings forward his own particular hypotheses concerning the interconnexions and aims of mental acts – all more or less plausible and all equally untrustworthy? There is an evident lack of any common foundation. And it is for that reason too that in the field of psychology there is, so to speak, no respect and no authority. In that field everyone can 'run wild' as he chooses. If you raise a question in physics or chemistry, anyone who knows he possesses no 'technical knowledge' will hold his tongue. But if you venture upon a psychological assertion you must be prepared to meet judgements and contradictions from every quarter. In this field, apparently, there is no 'technical knowledge'. Everyone has a mental life, so everyone regards himself as a psychologist. But that strikes me as an inadequate legal title. The story is told of how someone who applied for a post as a children's nurse was asked if she knew how to look after babies. 'Of course,' she replied, 'why, after all, I was a baby once myself.'

'And you claim that you have discovered this "common

foundation" of mental life, which has been overlooked by every psychologist, from observations on *sick
people* ?'

The source of our findings does not seem to me to deprive
them of their value. Embryology, to take an example,
would not deserve to be trusted if it could not give a plain
explanation of the origin of innate malformations. I have
told you of people whose thoughts go their own way, so
that they are obliged to worry over problems to which they
are perfectly indifferent. Do you think that academic
psychology could ever make the smallest contribution
towards explaining an abnormality such as that ? And, after
all, we all of us have the experience at night-time of our
thoughts going their own way and creating things which we
do not understand, which puzzle us, and which are suspi-
ciously reminiscent of pathological products. Our dreams, I
mean. The common people have always firmly believed that
dreams have a sense and a value – that they mean something. Academic psychology has never been able to inform
us what this meaning is. It could make nothing of dreams.
If it attempted to produce explanations, they were non-
psychological – such as tracing them to sensory stimuli, or
to an unequal depth of sleep in different portions of the
brain, and so on. But it is fair to say that a psychology
which cannot explain dreams is also useless for an understanding of normal mental life, that it has no claim to be
called a science.

'You are becoming agressive; so you have evidently got
on to a sensitive spot. I have heard, it is true, that in analysis
great value is attached to dreams, that they are interpreted,
and that memories of real events are looked for behind them,
and so on. But I have heard as well that the interpretation
of dreams is left to the caprice of analysts, and that they
themselves have never ceased disputing over the way of
interpreting dreams and the justification for drawing conclusions from them. If that is so, you ought not to underline

so heavily the advantage that analysis has won over academic psychology.'

There is really a great deal of truth in what you say. It is true that the interpretation of dreams has come to have unequalled importance both for the theory and the practice of analysis. If I seem to be aggressive, that is only a way of defending myself. And when I think of all the mischief some analysts have done with the interpretation of dreams I might lose heart and echo the pessimistic pronouncement of our great satirist Nestroy* when he says that every step forward is only half as big as it looks at first. But have you ever found that men do anything but confuse and distort what they get hold of? By the help of a little foresight and self-discipline most of the dangers of dream-interpretation can be avoided with certainty. But you will agree that I shall never come to my exposition if we let ourselves be led aside like this.

'Yes. If I understood rightly, you wanted to tell me about the fundamental postulate of the new psychology.'

That was not what I wanted to begin with. My purpose is to let you hear what pictures we have formed of the structure of the mental apparatus in the course of our analytic studies.

'What do you mean by the "mental apparatus"? and what, may I ask, is it constructed of?'

It will soon be clear what the mental apparatus is; but I must beg you not to ask what material it is constructed of. That is not a subject of psychological interest. Psychology can be as indifferent to it as, for instance, optics can be to the question of whether the walls of a telescope are made of metal or cardboard. We shall leave entirely on one side the *material* line of approach,† but not so the *spatial* one. For

---

*[Johann Nestroy (1801–62), famous in Vienna as a writer of comedies and farces.]

†[The question of what *material* the mental apparatus is constructed of.]

we picture the unknown apparatus which serves the activities of the mind as being really like an instrument constructed of several parts (which we speak of as 'agencies'), each of which performs a particular function and which have a fixed spatial relation to one another: it being understood that by spatial relation – 'in front of' and 'behind', 'superficial' and 'deep' – we merely mean in the first instance a representation of the regular succession of the functions. Have I made myself clear?

'Scarcely. Perhaps I shall understand it later. But, in any case, here is a strange anatomy of the soul – a thing which, after all, no longer exists at all for the scientists.'

What do you expect? It is a hypothesis like so many others in the sciences: the very earliest ones have always been rather rough. 'Open to revision' we can say in such cases. It seems to me unnecessary for me to appeal here to the 'as if' which has become so popular. The value of a 'fiction' of this kind (as the philosopher Vaihinger* would call it) depends on how much one can achieve with its help.

But to proceed. Putting ourselves on the footing of everyday knowledge, we recognize in human beings a mental organization which is interpolated between their sensory stimuli and the perception of their somatic needs on the one hand and their motor acts on the other, and which mediates between them for a particular purpose. We call this organization their '*Ich*' ['ego'; literally, 'I']. Now there is nothing new in this. Each one of us makes this assumption without being a philosopher, and some people even in spite of being philosophers. But this does not, in our opinion, exhaust the description of the mental apparatus. Besides this 'I', we recognize another mental region, more extensive, more

* [Hans Vaihinger (1852–1933). His philosophical system was enunciated in *Die Philosophie des Als Ob*, 1911. An English translation by C. K. Ogden appeared in 1924 under the title *The Philosophy of 'As if'*. The work had a considerable vogue in German-speaking countries, especially after the First World War.]

imposing, and more obscure than the 'I', and this we call the '*Es*' ['id'; literally, 'it']. The relation between the two must be our immediate concern.

You will probably protest at our having chosen simple pronouns to describe our two agencies or provinces instead of giving them orotund Greek names. In psycho-analysis, however, we like to keep in contact with the popular mode of thinking and prefer to make its concepts scientifically serviceable rather than to reject them. There is no merit in this; we are obliged to take this line; for our theories must be understood by our patients, who are often very intelligent, but not always learned. The impersonal 'it' is immediately connected with certain forms of expression used by normal people. 'It shot through me,' people say; 'there was something in me at that moment that was stronger than me.' '*C'était plus fort que moi.*'

In psychology we can only describe things by the help of analogies. There is nothing peculiar in this; it is the case elsewhere as well. But we have constantly to keep changing these analogies, for none of them lasts us long enough. Accordingly, in trying to make the relation between the ego and the id clear, I must ask you to picture the ego as a kind of façade of the id, as a frontage, like an external, cortical, layer of it. We can hold on to this last analogy. We know that cortical layers owe their peculiar characteristics to the modifying influence of the external medium on which they abut. Thus we suppose that the ego is the layer of the mental apparatus (of the id) which has been modified by the influence of the external world (of reality). This will show you how in psycho-analysis we take spatial ways of looking at things seriously. For us the ego is really something superficial and the id something deeper – looked at from outside, of course. The ego lies between reality and the id, which is what is truly mental.

'I will not ask any questions yet as to how all this can be known. But tell me first what you gain from this distinction between an ego and an id? What leads you to make it?'

Your question shows me the right way to proceed. For the important and valuable thing is to know that the ego and the id differ greatly from each other in several respects. The rules governing the course of mental acts are different in the ego and id; the ego pursues different purposes and by other methods. A great deal could be said about this; but perhaps you will be content with a fresh analogy and an example. Think of the difference between 'the front' and 'behind the lines', as things were during the war. We were not surprised then that some things were different at the front from what they were behind the lines, and that many things were permitted behind the lines which had to be forbidden at the front. The determining influence was, of course, the proximity of the enemy; in the case of mental life it is the proximity of the external world. There was a time when 'outside', 'strange', and 'hostile' were identical concepts. And now we come to the example. In the id there are no conflicts; contradictions and antitheses persist side by side in it unconcernedly, and are often adjusted by the formation of compromises. In similar circumstances the ego feels a conflict which must be decided; and the decision lies in one urge being abandoned in favour of the other. The ego is an organization characterized by a very remarkable trend towards unification, towards synthesis. This characteristic is lacking in the id; it is, as we might say, 'all to pieces'; its different urges pursue their own purposes independently and regardless of one another.

'And if such an important mental region "behind the lines" exists, how can you explain its having been overlooked till the time of analysis?'

That brings us back to one of your earlier questions [pp. 101–2]. Psychology had barred its own access to the region of the id by insisting on a postulate which is plausible enough but untenable: namely, that all mental acts are conscious* to us – that being conscious is the criterion of what is mental, and that, if there are processes in our brain which are not conscious, they do not deserve to be called mental acts and are no concern of psychology.

'But I should have thought that was obvious.'

Yes, and that is what psychologists think. Nevertheless it can easily be shown to be false – that is, to be a quite inexpedient distinction. The idlest self-observation shows that ideas may occur to us which cannot have come about without preparation. But you experience nothing of these preliminaries of your thought, though they too must certainly have been of a mental nature; all that enters your consciousness is the ready-made result. Occasionally you can make these preparatory thought-structures conscious *in retrospect*, as though in a reconstruction.

'Probably one's attention was distracted, so that one failed to notice the preparations.'

Evasions! You cannot in that way get around the fact that acts of a mental nature, and often very complicated ones, can take place in you, of which your consciousness learns nothing and of which you know nothing. Or are you prepared to suppose that a greater or smaller amount of your 'attention' is enough to transform a non-mental act into a mental one? But what is the use of disputing? There are hypnotic experiments in which the existence of such non-conscious thoughts are irrefutably demonstrated to anyone who cares to learn.

'I shall not retract; but I believe I understand you at last. What you call "ego" is consciousness; and your "id" is the so-called subconscious that people talk about so much nowadays. But why the masquerading with the new names?'

*[It should be remarked that the German word for 'conscious' – *bewusst* – has a passive form and is regularly used by Freud in a passive sense. Thus he would not as a rule speak of a person being conscious of a sensation but of a sensation being conscious to a person.]

It is not masquerading. The other names are of no use. And do not try to give me literature instead of science. If someone talks of subconsciousness, I cannot tell whether he means the term topographically – to indicate something lying in the mind beneath consciousness – or qualitatively – to indicate another consciousness, a subterranean one, as it were. He is probably not clear about any of it. The only trustworthy antithesis is between conscious and unconscious. But it would be a serious mistake to think that this antithesis coincides with the distinction between ego and id. Of course it would be delightful if it were as simple as that: our theory would have a smooth passage. But things are not so simple. All that is true is that everything that happens in the id is and remains unconscious, and that processes in the ego, and they alone, *can* become conscious. But not all of them are, nor always, nor necessarily; and large portions of the ego can remain permanently unconscious.

The becoming conscious of a mental process is a complicated affair. I cannot resist telling you – once again, dogmatically – our hypotheses about it. The ego, as you will remember, is the external, peripheral layer of the id. Now, we believe that on the outermost surface of this ego there is a special agency directed immediately to the external world, a system, an organ, through the excitation of which alone the phenomenon that we call consciousness comes about. This organ can be equally well excited from outside – thus receiving (with the help of the sense-organs) the stimuli from the external world – and from inside – thus becoming aware, first, of the sensations in the id, and then also of the processes in the ego.

'This is getting worse and worse and I can understand it less and less. After all, what you invited me to was a discussion of the question whether laymen (=non-doctors) ought to undertake analytic treatments. What is the point, then, of all these disquisitions on daring and obscure theories which you cannot convince me are justified?'

I know I cannot convince you. That is beyond any possibility and for that reason beyond my purpose. When we give our pupils theoretical instruction in psycho-analysis, we can see how little impression we are making on them to begin with. They take in the theories of analysis as coolly as other abstractions with which they are nourished. A few of them may perhaps *wish* to be convinced, but there is not a trace of their being so. But we also require that everyone who wants to practise analysis on other people shall first himself submit to an analysis. It is only in the course of this 'self-analysis' (as it is misleadingly termed),* when they actually experience as affecting their own person – or rather, their own mind – the processes asserted by analysis, that they acquire the convictions by which they are later guided as analysts. How then could I expect to convince you, the Impartial Person, of the correctness of our theories, when I can only put before you an abbreviated and therefore unintelligible account of them, without confirming them from your own experiences?

I am acting with a different purpose. The question at issue between us is not in the least whether analysis is sensible or nonsensical, whether it is right in its hypotheses or has fallen into gross errors. I am unrolling our theories before you since that is the best way of making clear to you what the range of ideas is that analysis embraces, on the basis of what hypotheses it approaches a patient and what it does with him. In this way a quite definite light will be thrown on the question of lay analysis. And do not be alarmed. If you have followed me so far you have got over the worst. Everything that follows will be easier for you. But now, with your leave, I will pause to take breath.

*[This is now usually described as a 'training analysis'.]

III

'I EXPECT you will want to tell me how, on the basis of the theories of psycho-analysis, the origin of a neurotic illness can be pictured.'

I will try to. But for that purpose we must study our ego and our id from a fresh angle, from the *dynamic* one – that is to say, having regard to the forces at work in them and between them. Hitherto we have been content with a *description* of the mental apparatus.

'My only fear is that it may become unintelligible again!'

I hope not. You will soon find your way about in it. Well then, we assume that the forces which drive the mental apparatus into activity are produced in the bodily organs as an expression of the major somatic needs. You will recollect the words of our poet philosopher: 'Hunger and love [are what moves the world].'* Incidentally, quite a formidable pair of forces! We give these bodily needs, in so far as they represent an instigation to mental activity, the name of '*Triebe*' [instincts], a word for which we are envied by many modern languages.† Well, these instincts fill the id: all the energy in the id, as we may put it briefly, originates from them. Nor have the forces in the ego any other origin; they are derived from those in the id. What, then, do these instincts want? Satisfaction – that is, the establishment of situations in which the bodily needs can be extinguished. A lowering of the tension of need is felt by our organ of consciousness as pleasurable; an increase of it is soon felt as unpleasure. From these oscillations arises the series of feelings of pleasure-unpleasure, in accordance with which the

* [Schiller, 'Die Weltweisen'.]
† [Various translations have been adopted for the word *Trieb*, the most literal being 'drive'.]

whole mental apparatus regulates its activity. In this connexion we speak of a 'dominance of the pleasure principle'.

If the id's instinctual demands meet with no satisfaction,
intolerable conditions arise. Experience soon shows that
these situations of satisfaction can only be established with
the help of the external world. At that point the portion of
the id which is directed towards the external world – the
ego – begins to function. If all the driving force that sets the
vehicle in motion is derived from the id, the ego, as it were,
undertakes the steering, without which no goal can be reached. The instincts in the id press for immediate satisfaction
at all costs, and in that way they achieve nothing or even
bring about appreciable damage. It is the task of the ego to
guard against such mishaps, to mediate between the claims
of the id and the objections of the external world. It carries
on its activity in two directions. On the one hand, it ob-
serves the external world with the help of its sense-organ,
the system of consciousness, so as to catch the favourable
moment for harmless satisfaction; and on the other hand it
influences the id, bridles its 'passions', induces its instincts
to postpone their satisfaction and, indeed, if the necessity
is recognized, to modify its aims, or, in return for some
compensation, to give them up. In so far as it tames the id's
impulses in this way, it replaces the pleasure principle,
which was formerly alone decisive, by what is known as the
'reality principle', which, though it pursues the same ultimate aims, takes into account the conditions imposed by
the real external world. Later, the ego learns that there is
yet another way of securing satisfaction besides the *adaptation* to the external world which I have described. It is also
possible to intervene in the external world by *changing* it,
and to establish in it intentionally the conditions which
make satisfaction possible. This activity then becomes the
ego's highest function; decisions as to when it is more expedient to control one's passions and bow before reality,
and when it is more expedient to side with them and to

take arms against the external world – such decisions make up the whole essence of worldly wisdom.

'And does the id put up with being dominated like this by the ego, in spite of being, if I understand you aright, the stronger party?'

Yes, all will be well if the ego is in possession of its whole organization and efficiency, if it has access to all parts of the id and can exercise its influence on them. For there is no natural opposition between ego and id; they belong together, and under healthy conditions cannot in practice be distinguished from each other.

'That sounds very pretty; but I cannot see how in such an ideal relation there can be the smallest room for a pathological disturbance.'

You are right. So long as the ego and its relations to the id fulfil these ideal conditions, there will be no neurotic disturbance. The point at which the illness makes its breach is an unexpected one, though no one acquainted with general pathology will be surprised to find a confirmation of the principle that it is precisely the most important developments and differentiations that carry in them the seeds of illness, of failure of function.

'You are becoming too learned. I cannot follow you.'

I must go back a little bit further. A small living organism is a truly miserable, powerless thing, is it not? compared with the immensely powerful external world, full as it is of destructive influences. A primitive organism, which has not developed any adequate ego-organization, is at the mercy of all these 'traumas'. It lives by the 'blind' satisfaction of its instinctual wishes and often perishes in consequence. The differentiation of an ego is above all a step towards self-preservation. Nothing, it is true, can be learnt from being destroyed; but if one has luckily survived a trauma one takes notice of the approach of similar situations and signalizes the danger by an abbreviated repetition of the impressions one has experienced in connexion with the trauma – by an *affect of anxiety*. This reaction to the perception of the danger now introduces an attempt at flight, which can have a life-saving effect till one has grown strong enough to meet the dangers of the external world in a more active fashion – even aggressively, perhaps.

'All this is very far away from what you promised to tell me.'

You have no notion how close I am to fulfilling my promise. Even in organisms which later develop an efficient ego-organization, their ego is feeble and little differentiated from their id to begin with, during their first years of childhood. Imagine now what will happen if this powerless ego experiences an instinctual demand from the id which it would already like to resist (because it senses that to satisfy it is dangerous and would conjure up a traumatic situation, a collision with the external world) but which it cannot control, because it does not yet possess enough strength to do so. In such a case the ego treats the instinctual danger as if it was an external one; it makes an attempt at flight, draws back from this portion of the id, and leaves it to its fate, after withholding from it all the contributions which it usually makes to instinctual impulses. The ego, as we put it, institutes a *repression* of these instinctual impulses. For the moment this has the effect of fending off the danger; but one cannot confuse the inside and the outside with impunity. One cannot run away from oneself. In repression the ego is following the pleasure principle, which it is usually in the habit of correcting; and it is bound to suffer damage in revenge. This lies in the ego's having permanently narrowed its sphere of influence. The repressed instinctual impulse is now isolated, left to itself, inaccessible, but also uninfluenceable. It goes its own way. Even later, as a rule, when the ego has grown stronger, it still cannot lift the repression; its synthesis is impaired, a part of the id remains forbidden ground to the ego. Nor does the isolated instinctual impulse remain idle; it understands how to make up for being denied normal satisfaction; it produces psychical derivatives which take its place; it links itself to other processes which by its influence it likewise tears away from the ego; and finally it breaks through into the ego and into consciousness in the form of an unrecognizably distorted substitute, and creates what we call a symptom. All at once the nature of a neurotic disorder becomes clear to us: on the one hand an ego which is inhibited in its synthesis, which has no influence on parts of the id, which must renounce some of its activities in order to avoid a fresh collision with what has been repressed, and which exhausts itself in what are for the most part vain acts of defence against the symptoms, the derivatives of the repressed impulses; and on the other hand an id in which individual instincts have made themselves independent, pursue their aims regardless of the interests of the person as a whole, and henceforth obey the laws only of the primitive psychology that rules in the depths of the id. If we survey the whole situation we arrive at a simple formula for the origin of a neurosis: the ego has made an attempt to suppress certain portions of the id *in an inappropriate manner*, this attempt has failed, and the id has taken its revenge. A neurosis is thus the result of a conflict between the ego and the id, upon which the ego has embarked because, as careful investigation shows, it wishes at all costs to retain its adaptability in relation to the real external world. The disagreement is between the external world and the id; and it is because the ego, loyal to its inmost nature, takes sides with the external world that it becomes involved in a conflict with its id. But please observe that what creates the determinant for the illness is not the fact of this conflict – for disagreements of this kind between reality and the id are unavoidable and it is one of the ego's standing tasks to mediate in them – but the circumstance that the ego has made use of the inefficient instrument of repression for dealing with the conflict. But this in turn is due to the fact that the ego, at the time at which it was set the task, was undeveloped and powerless. The decisive repressions all take place in early childhood.

'What a remarkable business! I shall follow your advice and not make criticisms, since you only want to show me what psycho-analysis believes about the origin of neurosis so that you can go on to say how it sets about combating it. I should have various questions to ask and later on I shall raise some of them. But at the moment I myself feel tempted for once to carry your train of thought further and to venture upon a theory of my own. You have expounded the relation between external world, ego, and id, and you have laid it down as the determinant of a neurosis that the ego in its dependence on the external world struggles against the id. Is not the opposite case conceivable of the ego in a conflict of this kind allowing itself to be dragged away by the id and disavowing its regard for the external world? What happens in a case like that? From my lay notions of the nature of insanity I should say that such a decision on the part of the ego might be the determinant of insanity. After all, a turning away of that kind from reality seems to be the essence of insanity.'

Yes. I myself have thought of that possibility, and indeed I believe it meets the facts – though to prove the suspicion true would call for a discussion of some highly complicated considerations. Neuroses and psychoses are evidently intimately related, but they must nevertheless differ in some decisive respect. That might well be the side taken by the ego in a conflict of this kind. In both cases the id would retain its characteristic of blind inflexibility.

'Well, go on! What hints on the treatment of neurotic illnesses does your theory give?'

It is easy now to describe our therapeutic aim. We try to restore the ego, to free it from its restrictions, and to give it back the command over the id which it has lost owing to its early repressions. It is for this one purpose that we carry out analysis, our whole technique is directed to this aim. We have to seek out the repressions which have been set up and to urge the ego to correct them with our help and to deal with conflicts better than by an attempt at flight. Since these repressions belong to the very early years of child-hood, the work of analysis leads us, too, back to that period. Our path to these situations of conflict, which have for the most part been forgotten and which we try to revive in the patient's memory, is pointed out to us by his symptoms, dreams, and free associations. These must, however, first be interpreted – translated – for, under the influence of the psychology of the id, they have assumed forms of expres-sion that are strange to our comprehension. We may assume that whatever associations, thoughts, and memories the pat-ient is unable to communicate to us without internal strug-gles are in some way connected with the repressed material or are its derivatives. By encouraging the patient to disre-gard his resistances to telling us these things, we are educat-ing his ego to overcome its inclination towards attempts at flight and to tolerate an approach to what is repressed. In the end, if the situation of the repression can be successfully reproduced in his memory, his compliance will be brilliantly rewarded. The whole difference between his age then and now works in his favour; and the thing from which his childish ego fled in terror will often seem to his adult and strengthened ego no more than child's play.

IV

'EVERYTHING you have told me so far has been psychology. It has often sounded strange, difficult, or obscure; but it has always been – if I may put it so – "pure". I have known very little hitherto, no doubt, about your psychoanalysis; but the rumour has nevertheless reached my ears that you are principally occupied with things that have no claim to that predicate. The fact that you have not yet touched on anything of the kind makes me feel that you are deliberately keeping something back. And there is another doubt that I cannot suppress. After all, as you yourself say, neuroses are disturbances of mental life. Is it possible, then, that such important things as our ethics, our conscience, our ideals, play no part at all in these profound disturbances?'

So you feel that a consideration both of what is lowest and of what is highest has been missing from our discussions up till now? The reason for that is that we have not yet considered the *contents* of mental life at all. But allow me now for once myself to play the part of an interrupter who holds up the progress of the conversation. I have talked so much psychology to you because I wanted you to get the impression that the work of analysis is a part of applied psychology – and, moreover, of a psychology that is unknown outside analysis. An analyst must therefore first and foremost have learnt this psychology, this depth-psychology or psychology of the unconscious, or as much of it at least as is known today. We shall need this as a basis for our later conclusions. But now, what was it you meant by your allusion to 'purity'?

'Well, it is generally reported that in analyses the most intimate – and the nastiest – events in sexual life come up for discussion in every detail. If that is so – I have not been able to gather from your psychological discussions that it is necessarily so – it would be a strong argument in favour of restricting these treatments to doctors. How could one dream of allowing such dangerous liberties to people of whose discretion one was not sure and of whose character one had no guarantee?'

It is true that doctors enjoy certain privileges in the sphere of sex: they are even allowed to inspect people's genitals – though they were not allowed to in the East and though some idealistic reformers (you know whom I have in mind)* have disputed this privilege. But you want to know in the first place whether it is so in analysis and why it must be so. Yes, it is so.

And it must be so, firstly because analysis is entirely founded on complete candour. Financial circumstances, for instance, are discussed with equal detail and openness: things are said that are kept back from every fellow-citizen, even if he is not a competitor or a tax-collector. I will not dispute – indeed, I will myself insist with energy – that this obligation to candour puts a grave moral responsibility on the analyst as well. And it must be so, secondly, because factors from sexual life play an extremely important, a dominating, perhaps even a *specific*, part among the causes and precipitating factors of neurotic illnesses. What else can analysis do but keep close to its subject-matter, to the material brought up by the patient? The analyst never entices his patient on to the ground of sex. He does not say to him in advance: 'We shall be dealing with the intimacies of your sexual life!' He allows him to begin what he has to say wherever he pleases, and quietly waits until the patient himself touches on sexual things. I used always to warn my pupils: 'Our opponents have told us that we shall come upon cases in which the factor of sex plays no part. Let us be careful not to introduce it into our analyses and so spoil

*[No doubt Tolstoy and his followers.]

our chance of finding such a case.' But so far none of us has had that good fortune.

I am aware, of course, that our recognition of sexuality has become – whether admittedly or not – the strongest motive for other people's hostility to analysis. Can that shake our confidence ? It merely shows us how neurotic our whole civilized life is, since ostensibly normal people do not behave very differently from neurotics. At a time when psycho-analysis was solemnly put on its trial before the learned societies of Germany – today things have grown altogether quieter – one of the speakers claimed to possess peculiar authority because, so he said, he even allowed his patients to talk : for diagnostic purposes, clearly, and to test the assertions of analysts. 'But', he added, 'if they begin to talk about sexual matters I shut their mouths.' What do you think of that as a method of demonstration ? The learned society applauded the speaker to the echo instead of feeling suitably ashamed on his account. Only the triumphant certainty afforded by the consciousness of prejudices held in common can explain this speaker's want of logical thought. Years later a few of those who had at that time been my followers gave in to the need to free human society from the yoke of sexuality which psycho-analysis was seeking to impose on it. One of them explained that what is sexual does not mean sexuality at all, but something else, something abstract and mystical. And another actually declared that sexual life is merely one of the spheres in which human beings seek to put in action their driving need for power and domination. They have met with much applause, for the moment at least.

'I shall venture, for once in a way, to take sides on that point. It strikes me as extremely bold to assert that sexuality is not a natural, primitive need of living organisms, but an expression of something else. One need only take the example of animals.'

That makes no difference. There is no mixture, however

absurd, that society will not willingly swallow down if it is advertised as an antidote to the dreaded predominance of sexuality.

I confess, moreover, that the dislike that you yourself have betrayed of assigning to the factor of sexuality so great a part in the causation of neurosis – I confess that this scarcely seems to me consistent with your task as an Impartial Person. Are you not afraid that this antipathy may interfere with your passing judgement?

'I'm sorry to hear you say that. Your reliance on me seems to be shaken. But in that case why not have chosen someone else as your Impartial Person?'

Because that someone else would not have thought any differently from you. But if he had been prepared from the first to recognize the importance of sexual life, everyone would have exclaimed: 'Why, that is no Impartial Person, he is one of your supporters!' No, I am far from abandoning the expectation of being able to influence your opinions. I must admit, however, that from my point of view this situation is different from the one we dealt with earlier. As regards our psychological discussions it is a matter of indifference to me whether you believe me or not, provided only that you get an impression that what we are concerned with are purely psychological problems. But here, as regards the question of sexuality, I should nevertheless be glad if you were accessible to the realization that your strongest motive for contradiction is precisely the ingrained hostility which you share with so many other people.

'But after all I am without the experience that has given you your unshakeable certainty.'

Very well. I can now proceed with my exposition. Sexual life is not simply something spicy; it is also a serious scientific problem. There was much that was novel to be learnt about it, many strange things to be explained. I told you just now that analysis has to go back into the early years of the patient's childhood, because the decisive repressions have taken place then, while his ego was feeble. But surely in childhood there is no sexual life ? surely it only starts at puberty ? On the contrary. We have to learn that sexual instinctual impulses accompany life from birth onwards, and that it is precisely in order to fend off those instincts that the infantile ego institutes repressions. A remarkable coincidence, is it not ? that small children should already be struggling against the power of sexuality, just as the speaker in the learned society was to do later, and later still my followers who have set up their own theories. How does that come about ? The most general explanation would be that our civilization is built up entirely at the expense of sexuality; but there is much more to be said on the subject.

The discovery of infantile sexuality is one of those of which we have reason to feel ashamed [because of its obviousness]. A few paediatricians have, it seems, always known about it, and a few children's nurses. Clever men, who call theselves child psychologists, have thereupon spoken in tones of reproach of a 'desecration of the in-nocence of childhood'. Once again, sentiment instead of argument ! Events of that kind are of daily occurrence in political bodies. A member of the Opposition rises and denounces some piece of maladministration in the Civil Service, in the Army, in the Judiciary, and so on. Upon this another member, preferably one of the Government, de-clares that such statements are an affront to the sense of honour of the body politic, of the army, of the dynasty, or even of the nation. So they are as good as untrue. Feelings such as these can tolerate no affronts.

The sexual life of children is of course different from that of adults. The sexual function, from its beginnings to the definitive form in which it is so familiar to us, undergoes a complicated process of development. It grows together from numerous component instincts with different aims and passes through several phases of organization till at last it come into the service of reproduction. Not all the

component instincts are equally serviceable for the final
outcome; they must be diverted, remodelled, and in part
suppressed. Such a far-reaching course of development is
not always passed through without a flaw; inhibitions in
development take place, partial fixations at early stages of
development. If obstacles arise later on to the exercise of
the sexual function, the sexual urge – the libido, as we call
it – is apt to hark back to these earlier points of fixation.
The study of the sexuality of children and its transforma-
tions up to maturity has also given us the key to an understanding of what are known as the sexual perversions, which
people used always to describe with all the requisite indica-
tions of disgust but whose origin they were never able to
explain. The whole topic is of uncommon interest, but for
the purposes of our conversation there is not much sense
in telling you more about it. To find one's way about in it
one of course needs anatomical and physiological knowledge, all of which is unfortunately not to be acquired in
medical schools. But a familiarity with the history of
civilization and with mythology is equally indispensable.

'After all that, I still cannot form any picture of the
sexual life of children.'

Then I will pursue the subject further; in any case it is
not easy for me to get away from it. I will tell you, then,
that the most remarkable thing about the sexual life of
children seems to me that it passes through the whole of its
very far-reaching development in the first five years of life.
From then onwards until puberty there stretches what is
known as the period of latency. During it sexuality normally advances no further; on the contrary, the sexual urges
diminish in strength and many things are given up and
forgotten which the child did and knew. During that period
of life, after the early efflorescence of sexuality has
withered, such attitudes of the ego as shame, disgust, and
morality arise, which are destined to stand up against the
later tempest of puberty and to lay down the path of the

freshly awakening sexual desires. This 'diphasic onset',* as it is named, of sexual life has a great deal to do with the genesis of neurotic illnesses. It seems to occur only in human beings, and it is perhaps one of the determinants of the human privilege of becoming neurotic. The prehistory of sexual life was just as much overlooked before psycho-analysis as, in another department, the background to conscious mental life. You will rightly suspect that the two are intimately connected.

There is much to be told, for which our expectations have not prepared us, about the contents, manifestations, and achievements of this early period of sexuality. For instance, you will no doubt be surprised to hear how often little boys are afraid of being eaten up by their father. (And you may also be surprised at my including this fear among the phenomena of sexual life.) But I may remind you of the mythological tale which you may still recall from your schooldays of how the god Kronos swallowed his children. How strange this must have sounded to you when you first heard it! But I suppose none of us thought about it at the time. Today we can also call to mind a number of fairy tales in which some ravenous animal like a wolf appears, and we shall recognize it as a disguise of the father. And this is an opportunity of assuring you that it was only through the knowledge of infantile sexuality that it became possible to understand mythology and the world of fairy tales. Here then something has been gained as a by-product of analytic studies.

You will be no less surprised to hear that male children suffer from a fear of being robbed of their sexual organ by their father, so that this fear of being castrated has a most powerful influence on the development of their character and in deciding the direction to be followed by their sexuality. And here again mythology may give you the courage to believe psycho-analysis. The same Kronos who

* [Onset in two waves.]

swallowed his children also emasculated his father Uranus, and was afterwards himself emasculated in revenge by his son Zeus, who had been rescued through his mother's cunning. If you have felt inclined to suppose that all that psycho-analysis reports about the early sexuality of children is derived from the disordered imagination of the analysts, you must at least admit that their imagination has created the same product as the imaginative activities of primitive man, of which myths and fairy tales are the precipitate. The alternative friendlier, and probably also the more pertinent, view would be that in the mental life of children today we can still detect the same archaic factors which were once dominant generally in the primeval days of human civilization. In his mental development the child would be repeating the history of his race in an abbreviated form, just as embryology long since recognized was the case with somatic development.

Another characteristic of early infantile sexuality is that the female sexual organ proper as yet plays no part in it: the child has not yet discovered it. Stress falls entirely on the male organ, all the child's interest is directed towards the question of whether it is present or not. We know less about the sexual life of little girls than of boys. But we need not feel ashamed of this distinction; after all, the sexual life of adult women is a 'dark continent' for psychology. But we have learnt that girls feel deeply their lack of a sexual organ that is equal in value to the male one; they regard themselves on that account as inferior, and this 'envy for the penis' is the origin of a whole number of characteristic feminine reactions.

It is also characteristic of children that their two excretory needs are cathected [charged] with sexual interest. Later on, education draws a sharp distinction here, which is once more obliterated in the practice of joking. It may seem to us an unsavoury fact, but it takes quite a long time for children to develop feelings of disgust. This is not disputed even by people who insist otherwise on the seraphic purity of the child's mind.

Nothing, however, deserves more notice than the fact that children regularly direct their sexual wishes towards their nearest relatives – in the first place, therefore, towards their father and mother, and afterwards towards their brothers and sisters. The first object of a boy's love is his mother, and of a girl's her father (except in so far as an innate bisexual disposition favours the simultaneous presence of the contrary attitude). The other parent is felt as a disturbing rival and not infrequently viewed with strong hostility. You must understand me aright. What I mean to say is not that the child wants to be treated by its favourite parent merely with the kind of affection which we adults like to regard as the essence of the parent-child relation. No, analysis leaves us in no doubt that the child's wishes extend beyond such affection to all that we understand by sensual satisfaction – so far, that is, as the child's powers of imagination allow. It is easy to see that the child never guesses the actual facts of sexual intercourse; he replaces them by other notions derived from his own experience and feelings. As a rule his wishes culminate in the intention to bear, or in some indefinable way to procreate, a baby. Boys, too, in their ignorance, do not exclude themselves from the wish to bear a baby. We give the whole of this mental structure the name of 'Oedipus complex', after the familiar Greek legend. With the end of the early sexual period it should normally be given up, should radically disintegrate and become transformed; and the products of this transformation are destined for important functions in later mental life. But as a rule this is not effected radically enough, in which case puberty brings about a revival of the complex, which may have serious consequences.

I am surprised that you are still silent. That can scarcely mean consent. In asserting that a child's first choice of an object is, to use the technical term, an incestuous one, analysis no doubt once more hurt the most sacred feelings of humanity, and might well be prepared for a corresponding amount of disbelief, contradiction, and attack. And these it has received in abundance. Nothing has damaged it more in the good opinion of its contemporaries than its hypothesis of the Oedipus complex as a structure universally bound to human destiny. The Greek myth, incidentally, must have had the same meaning; but the majority of men today, learned and unlearned alike, prefer to believe that Nature has laid down an innate abhorrence in us as a guard against the possibility of incest.

But let us first summon history to our aid. When Caius Julius Caesar landed in Egypt, he found the young Queen Cleopatra (who was soon to become so important to him) married to her still younger brother Ptolemy. In an Egyptian dynasty there was nothing peculiar in this; the Ptolemies, who were of Greek origin, had merely carried on the custom which had been practised by their predecessors, the ancient Pharaohs, for a few thousand years. This, however, was merely brother-and-sister incest, which even at the present time is not judged so harshly. So let us turn to our chief witness in matters concerning primeval times – mythology. It informs us that the myths of every people, and not only of the Greeks, are filled with examples of love-affairs between fathers and daughters and even between mothers and sons. Cosmology, no less than the genealogy of royal races, is founded upon incest. For what purpose do you suppose these legends were created? To brand gods and kings as criminals? to fasten on them the abhorrence of the human race? Rather, surely, because incestuous wishes are a primordial human heritage and have never been fully overcome, so that their fulfilment was still granted to gods and their descendants when the majority of common humans were already obliged to renounce them. It is in complete harmony with these lessons of history and mythology that we find incestuous wishes still present and operative in the childhood of the individual.

'I might take it amiss that you tried to keep back all this about infantile sexuality from me. It seems to me most interesting, particularly on account of its connexion with human pre-history.'

I was afraid it might take us too far from our purpose. But perhaps after all it will be of use.

'Now tell me, though, what certainty can you offer for your analytic findings on the sexual life of children? Is your conviction based solely on points of agreement with mythology and history?'

Oh, by no means. It is based on direct observation. What happened was this. We had begun by inferring the content of sexual childhood from the analysis of adults – that is to say, some twenty or forty years later. Afterwards, we undertook analysis on children themselves, and it was no small triumph when we were thus able to confirm in them everything that we had been able to divine, in spite of the amount to which it had been overlaid and distorted in the interval.

'What? You have had small children in analysis? children of less than six years? *Can* that be done? And is it not most risky for the children?'

It can be done very well. It is hardly to be believed what goes on in a child of four or five years old. Children are very active-minded at that age; their early sexual period is also a period of intellectual flowering. I have an impression that with the onset of the latency period they become mentally inhibited as well, stupider. From that time on, too, many children lose their physical charm. And, as regards the damage done by early analysis, I may inform you that the first child on whom the experiment was ventured, nearly twenty years ago, has since then grown into a healthy and capable young man, who has passed through his puberty irreproachably, in spite of some severe psychical traumas.

It may be hoped that things will turn out no worse for the other 'victims' of early analysis. Much that is of interest attaches to these child analyses; it is possible that in the future they will become still more important. From the point of view of theory, their value is beyond question. They give unambiguous information on problems which remain unsolved in the analyses of adults; and they thus protect the analyst from errors that might have momentous consequences for him. One surprises the factors that lead to the formation of a neurosis while they are actually at work and one cannot then mistake them. In the child's interest, it is true, analytic influence must be combined with educational measures. The technique has still to receive its shaping. But practical interest is aroused by the observation that a very large number of our children pass through a plainly neurotic phase in the course of their development. Since we have learnt how to look more sharply, we are tempted to say that neurosis in children is not the exception but the rule, as though it could scarcely be avoided on the path from the innate disposition of infancy to civilized society. In most cases this neurotic phase in childhood is overcome spontaneously. But may it not also regularly leave its traces in the average healthy adult ? On the other hand in those who are neurotics in later life we never fail to find links with the illness in childhood, though at the time it need not have been very noticeable. In a precisely analogous way physicians today, I believe, hold the view that each one of us has gone through an attack of tuberculosis in his childhood. It is true that in the case of the neurosis the factor of immunization does not operate, but only the factor of predisposition.

Let me return to your question about certainty. We have become quite generally convinced from the direct analytic examination of children that we were right in our interpretation of what adults told us about their childhood. In a number of cases, however, another sort of confirmation has become possible. The material of the analysis of some patients has enabled us to reconstruct certain external happenings, certain impressive events of their childhood years, of which they have preserved no conscious memory. Lucky accidents, information from parents or nurses, have afterwards provided irrefutable evidence that these occurrences which we had inferred really did take place. This, of course, has not happened often, but when it has it has made an overwhelming impression. The correct reconstruction, you must know, of such forgotten experiences of childhood always has a great therapeutic effect, whether they permit of objective confirmation or not. These events owe their importance, of course, to their having occurred at such an early age, at a time when they could still produce a traumatic effect on the feeble ego.

'And what sort of events can these be, that have to be discovered by analysis?'

Various sorts. In the first place, impressions capable of permanently influencing the child's budding sexual life – such as observations of sexual activities between adults, or sexual experiences of his own with an adult or another child (no rare events); or, again, overhearing conversations, understood either at the time or retrospectively, from which the child thought it could draw conclusions about mysterious or uncanny matters; or again, remarks or actions by the child himself which give evidence of significant attitudes of affection or enmity towards other people. It is of special importance in an analysis to induce a memory of the patient's own forgotten sexual activity as a child and also of the intervention by the adults which brought it to an end.

'That gives me an opportunity to bring up a question that I have long wanted to ask. What, then, is the nature of this "sexual activity" of children at an early age, which, as you say, was overlooked before the days of analysis?'

It is an odd thing that the regular and essential part of this sexual activity was *not* overlooked. Or rather, it is by no means odd; for it was impossible to overlook it. Children's sexual impulses find their main expressions in self-gratification by friction of their own genitals, or, more precisely, of the male portion of them. The extraordinarly wide distribution of this form of childish 'naughtiness' was always known to adults, and it was regarded as a grave sin and severely punished. But please do not ask me how people could reconcile these observations of the immoral inclinations of children – for children do it, as they themselves say, because it gives them pleasure – with the theory of their innate purity and non-sensuality. You must get our opponents to solve this riddle. *We* have a more important problem before us. What attitude should we adopt towards the sexual activity of early childhood? We know the responsibility we are incurring if we suppress it; but we do not venture to let it take its course without restriction. Among races at a low level of civilization, and among the lower strata of civilized races, the sexuality of children seems to be given free rein. This probably provides a powerful protection against the subsequent development of neuroses in the individual. But does it not at the same time involve an extraordinary loss of the aptitude for cultural achievements? There is a good deal to suggest that here we are faced by a new Scylla and Charybdis.

But whether the interests which are stimulated by the study of the sexual life of neurotics create an atmosphere favourable to the encouragement of lasciviousness – *that* is a question which I venture to leave to your own judgement.

V

'I BELIEVE I understand your purpose. You want to show me what kind of knowledge is needed in order to practise analysis, so that I may be able to judge whether only doctors should have a right to do so. Well, so far very little to do with medicine has turned up: a great deal of psychology and a little biology or sexual science. But perhaps we have not got to the end ?'

Decidedly not. There are still gaps to be filled. May I make a request ? Will you describe how you now picture an analytic treatment ? – just as though you had to undertake one yourself.

'A fine idea, to be sure ! No, I have not the least intention of settling our controversy by an experiment of that sort. But just to oblige, I will do what you ask – the responsibility will be yours. Very well. I will suppose that the patient comes to me and complains of his troubles. I promise him recovery or improvement if he will follow my directions. I call on him to tell me with perfect candour everything that he knows and that occurs to him, and not to be deterred from that intention even if some things are disagreeable to say. Have I taken in the rule properly ?'

Yes. You should add : 'even if what occurs to him seems unimportant or senseless.'

'I will add that. Thereupon he begins to talk and I listen. And what then ? I infer from what he tells me the kind of impressions, experiences, and wishes which he has repressed because he came across them at a time when his ego was still feeble and was afraid of them instead of dealing with them. When he has learnt this from me, he puts himself back in the old situations and with my help he manages better. The limitations to which his ego was tied then disappear, and he is cured. Is that right ?'

Bravo ! bravo ! I see that once again people will be able to accuse me of having made an analyst of someone who is not a doctor. You have mastered it all admirably.

'I have done no more than repeat what I have heard from you – as though it was something I had learnt by heart. All the same, I cannot form any picture of how I should do it, and I am at quite a loss to understand why a job like that should take an hour a day for so many months. After all, an ordinary person has not as a rule experienced such a lot, and what was repressed in childhood is probably in every case the same.'

When one really practises analysis one learns all kinds of things besides. For instance : you would not find it at all such a simple matter to deduce from what the patient tells you the experiences he has forgotten and the instinctual impulses he has repressed. He says something to you which at first means as little to you as it does to him. You will have to make up your mind to look at the material which he delivers to you in obedience to the rule in a quite special way : as though it were ore, perhaps, from which its content of precious metal has to be extracted by a particular process. You will be prepared, too, to work over many tons of ore which may contain but little of the valuable material you are in search of. Here we should have a first reason for the prolonged character of the treatment.

'But how does one work over this raw material – to keep to your simile ?'

By assuming that the patient's remarks and associations are only distortions of what you are looking for – allusions, as it were, from which you have to guess what is hidden behind them. In a word, this material, whether it consists of memories, associations, or dreams, has first to be *interpreted*. You will do this, of course, with an eye to the expectations you have formed as you listened, thanks to your special knowledge.

' "Interpret!" A nasty word! I dislike the sound of it; it robs me of all certainty. If everything depends on my interpretation who can guarantee that I interpret right? So after all everything *is* left to my caprice.'

Just a moment! Things are not quite as bad as that. Why do you choose to except your own mental processes from the rule of law which you recognize in other people's? When you have attained some degree of self-discipline and have certain knowledge at your disposal, your interpretations will be independent of your personal characteristics and will hit the mark. I am not saying that the analyst's personality is a matter of indifference for this portion of his task. A kind of sharpness of hearing for what is unconscious and repressed, which is not possessed equally by everyone, has a part to play. And here, above all, we are brought to the analyst's obligation to make himself capable, by a deep-going analysis of his own, of the unprejudiced reception of the analytic material. Something, it is true, still remains over: something comparable to the 'personal equation' in astronomical observations. This individual factor will always play a larger part in psycho-analysis than elsewhere. An abnormal person can become an accurate physicist; as an analyst he will be hampered by his own abnormality from seeing the pictures of mental life undistorted. Since it is impossible to demonstrate to anyone his own abnormality, general agreement in matters of depth-psychology will be particularly hard to reach. Some psychologists, indeed, think it is quite impossible and that every fool has an equal right to give out his folly as wisdom. I confess that I am more of an optimist about this. After all, our experiences show that fairly satisfactory agreements can be reached even in psychology. Every field of research has its particular difficulty which we must try to eliminate. And, moreover, even in the interpretative art of analysis there

is much that can be learnt like any other material of study:
for instance, in connexion with the peculiar method of
indirect representation through symbols.

'Well, I no longer have any desire to undertake an
analytic treatment even in my imagination. Who can say
what other surprises I might meet with?'

You are quite right to give up the notion. You see how
much more training and practice would be needed. When
you have found the right interpretation, another task lies
ahead. You must wait for the right moment at which you
can communicate your interpretation to the patient with
some prospect of success.

'How can one always tell the right moment?'

That is a question of tact, which can become more refined
with experience. You will be making a bad mistake if, in
an effort, perhaps, at shortening the analysis, you throw
your interpretations at the patient's head as soon as you have
found them. In that way you will draw expressions of
resistance, rejection, and indignation from him; but you
will not enable his ego to master his repressed material. The
formula is: to wait till he has come so near to the repressed
material that he has only a few more steps to take under
the lead of the interpretation you propose.

'I believe I should never learn to do that. And if I carry
out these precautions in making my interpretation, what
next?'

It will then be your fate to make a discovery for which
you were not prepared.

'And what may that be?'

That you have been deceived in your patient; that you
cannot count in the slightest on his collaboration and compliance; that he is ready to place every possible difficulty in
the way of your common work – in a word, that he has
no wish whatever to be cured.

'Well! that is the craziest thing you have told me yet.
And I do not believe it either. The patient who is suffering

so much, who complains so movingly about his troubles, who is making so great a sacrifice for the treatment – you say he has no wish to be cured ! But of course you do not mean what you say.'

Calm yourself ! I *do* mean it. What I said was the truth – not the whole truth, no doubt, but a very noteworthy part of it. The patient wants to be cured – but he also wants not to be. His ego has lost its unity, and for that reason his will has no unity either. If that were not so, he would be no neurotic.

' "Were I sagacious, I should not be Tell !" '*

The derivatives of what is repressed have broken into his ego and established themselves there; and the ego has as little control over trends from that source as it has over what is actually repressed, and as a rule it knows nothing about them. These patients, indeed, are of a peculiar nature and raise difficulties with which we are not accustomed to reckon. All our social institutions are framed for people with a united and normal ego, which one can classify as good or bad, which either fufills its function or is altogether eliminated by an overpowering influence. Hence the juridical alternative : responsible or irresponsible. None of these distinctions apply to neurotics. It must be admitted that there is difficulty in adapting social demands to their psychological condition. This was experienced on a large scale during the last war. Were the neurotics who evaded service malingerers or not? They were both. If they were treated as malingerers and if their illness was made highly uncomfortable, they recovered; if after being ostensibly restored they were sent back into service, they promptly took flight once more into illness. Nothing could be done with them. And the same is true of neurotics in civil life. They complain of their illness but exploit it with all their strength; and if someone tries to take it away from them they defend it like the proverbial lioness with her young. Yet there

* [Schiller, *Wilhelm Tell*, Act III, Scene 3.]

would be no sense in reproaching them for this contradiction.

'But would not the best plan be not to give these difficult people any treatment at all, but to leave them to themselves? I cannot think it is worth while to expend such great efforts over each of them as you lead me to suppose that you make.'

I cannot approve of your suggestion. It is undoubtedly a more proper line to accept the complications of life rather than struggle against them. It may be true that not every neurotic whom we treat is worth the expenditure of an analysis; but there are some very valuable individuals among them as well. We must set ourselves the goal of bringing it about that as few human beings as possible enter civilized life with such a defective mental equipment. And for that purpose we must collect much experience and learn to understand many things. Every analysis can be instructive and bring us a yield of new understanding quite apart from the personal value of the individual patient.

'But if a volitional impulse has been formed in the patient's ego which wishes to retain the illness, it too must have its reasons and motives and be able in some ways to justify itself. But it is impossible to see why anyone should want to be ill or what he can get out of it.'

Oh, that is not so hard to understand. Think of the war neurotics, who do not have to serve, precisely because they are ill. In civil life illness can be used as a screen to gloss over incompetence in one's profession or in competition with other people; while in the family it can serve as a means for sacrificing the other members and extorting proofs of their love or for imposing one's will upon them. All of this lies fairly near the surface; we sum it up in the term 'gain from illness'. It is curious, however, that the patient – that is, his ego – nevertheless knows nothing of the whole concatenation of these motives and the actions which they involve. One combats the influence of these trends by compelling the ego to take cognizance of them. But there are other motives, that lie still deeper, for holding on to being ill, which are not so easily dealt with. But these cannot be understood without a fresh journey into psychological theory.

'Please go on. A little more theory will make no odds now.'

When I described the relation between the ego and the id to you, I suppressed an important part of the theory of the mental apparatus. For we have been obliged to assume that within the ego itself a particular agency has become differentiated, which we name the super-ego. This super-ego occupies a special position between the ego and the id. It belongs to the ego and shares its high degree of psychological organization; but it has a particularly intimate connexion with the id. It is in fact a precipitate of the first object-cathexes of the id and is the heir to the Oedipus complex after its demise.* This super-ego can confront the ego and treat it like an object; and it often treats it very harshly. It is as important for the ego to remain on good terms with the super-ego as with the id. Estrangements between the ego and the super-ego are of great significance in mental life. You will already have guessed that the super-ego is the vehicle of the phenomenon that we call conscience. Mental health very much depends on the super-ego's being normally developed – that is, on its having become sufficiently impersonal. And that is precisely what it is not in neurotics, whose Oedipus complex has not passed through the correct process of transformation. Their super-ego still confronts their ego as a strict father confronts a child; and their morality operates in a primitive fashion

---

*[The charges of energy (cathexes) directed from the id on to its first external objects (the parents) are transformed into identifications and the objects are introduced into the ego and there take the form of a super-ego.]

in that the ego gets itself punished by the super-ego. Illness is employed as an instrument for this 'self-punishment', and neurotics have to behave as though they were governed by a sense of guilt which, in order to be satisfied, needs to be punished by illness.

'That really sounds most mysterious. The strangest thing about it is that apparently even this mighty force of the patient's conscience does not reach his consciousness.'

Yes, we are only beginning to appreciate the significance of all these important circumstances. That is why my description was bound to turn out so obscure. But now I can proceed. We describe all the forces that oppose the work of recovery as the patient's 'resistances'. The gain from illness is one such resistance. The 'unconscious sense of guilt' represents the super-ego's resistance; it is the most powerful factor, and the one most dreaded by us. We meet with still other resistances during the treatment. If the ego during the early period has set up a repression out of fear, then the fear still persists and manifests itself as a resistance if the ego approaches the repressed material. And finally, as you can imagine, there are likely to be difficulties if an instinctual process which has been going along a particular path for whole decades is suddenly expected to take a new path that has just been made open for it. That might be called the id's resistance. The struggle against all these resistances is our main work during an analytic treatment; the task of making interpretations is nothing compared to it. But as a result of this struggle and of the overcoming of the resistances, the patient's ego is so much altered and strengthened that we can look forward calmly to his future behaviour when the treatment is over. On the other hand, you can understand now why we need such long treatments. The length of the path of development and the wealth of the material are not the decisive factors. It is more a question of whether the path is clear. An army can be held up for weeks on a stretch of country which in peace time an express crosses in a couple of hours – if the army has to overcome the enemy's resistance there. Such battles call for time in mental life too. I am unfortunately obliged to tell you that every effort to hasten analytic treatment appreciably has hitherto failed. The best way of shortening it seems to be to carry it out according to the rules.

'If I ever felt any desire to poach on your preserves and try my hand at analysing someone else, what you tell me about the resistances would have cured me of it. But how about the special personal influence that you yourself have after all admitted? Does not that come into action against the resistances?'

It is a good thing you have asked me about that. This personal influence is our most powerful dynamic weapon. It is the new element which we introduce into the situation and by means of which we make it fluid. The intellectual content of our explanations cannot do it, for the patient, who shares all the prejudices of the world around him, need believe us as little as our scientific critics do. The neurotic sets to work because he has faith in the analyst, and he believes him because he acquires a special emotional attitude towards the figure of the analyst. Children, too, only believe people they are attached to. I have already told you [p. 101] what use we make of this particularly large 'suggestive' influence. Not for suppressing the symptoms – that distinguishes the analytic method from other psychotherapeutic procedures – but as a motive force to induce the patient to overcome his resistances.

'Well, and if that succeeds, does not everything then go smoothly?'

Yes, it ought to. But there turns out to be an unexpected complication. It was perhaps the greatest of the analyst's surprises to find that the emotional relation which the patient adopts towards him is of a quite peculiar nature. The very first doctor who attempted an analysis – it was not myself – came up against this phenomenon and did not know what to make of it. For this emotional relation is, to put it plainly, in the nature of falling in love. Strange, is it not ? Especially when you take into account that the analyst does nothing to provoke it but on the contrary rather keeps at a distance from the patient, speaking humanly, and surrounds himself with some degree of reserve – when you learn besides that this odd love-relationship disregards anything else that is really propitious and every variation in personal attraction, age, sex, or class. This love is of a positively compulsive kind. Not that that characteristic need be absent from spontaneous falling in love. As you know, the contrary is often the case. But in the analytic situation it makes its appearance with complete regularity without there being any rational explanation for it. One would have thought that the patient's relation to the analyst called for no more than a certain amount of respect, trust, gratitude, and human sympathy. Instead, there is this falling in love, which itself gives the impression of being a pathological phenomenon.

'I should have thought all the same that it would be favourable for your analytic purposes. If someone is in love, he is amenable, and he will do anything in the world for the sake of the other person.'

Yes. It *is* favourable to start with. But when this falling in love has grown deeper, its whole nature comes to light, much of which is incompatible with the task of analysis. The patient's love is not satisfied with being obedient; it grows exacting, calls for affectionate and sensual satisfactions, it demands exclusiveness, it develops jealousy, and it shows more and more clearly its reverse side, its readiness to become hostile and revengeful if it cannot obtain its ends. At the same time, like all falling in love, it drives away all other mental material; it extinguishes interest in the treatment and in recovery – in short, there can be no doubt that it has taken the place of the neurosis and that our work has had the result of driving out one form of illness with another.

'That does sound hopeless! What can be done about it? The analysis would have to be given up. But if, as you say, the same thing happens in every case, it would be impossible to carry through any analyses at all.'

We will begin by using the situation in order to learn something from it. What we learn may then perhaps help us to master it. Is it not an extremely noteworthy fact that we succeed in transforming every neurosis, whatever its content, into a condition of pathological love?

Our conviction that a portion of erotic life that has been abnormally employed lies at the basis of neuroses must be unshakeably strengthened by this experience. With this discovery we are once more on a firm footing and can venture to make this love itself the object of analysis. And we can make another observation. Analytic love is not manifested in every case as clearly and blatantly as I have tried to depict it. Why not? We can soon see. In proportion as the purely sensual and the hostile sides of his love try to show themselves the patient's opposition to them is aroused. He struggles against them and tries to repress them before our very eyes. And now we understand what is happening. The patient is *repeating* in the form of falling in love with the analyst mental experiences which he has already been through once before; he has *transferred* on to the analyst mental attitudes that were lying ready in him and were intimately connected with his neurosis. He is also repeating before our eyes his old defensive actions; he would like best to repeat in his relation to the analyst *all* the history of that forgotten period of his life. So what he is showing us is the kernel of his intimate life history: *he is reproducing it tangibly, as though it were actually happening, instead of remembering it.* In this way the riddle of the transference-love is solved and the analysis can proceed on its way – with the *help* of the new situation which had seemed such a menace to it.

'That is very cunning. And is the patient so easy to convince that he is not in love but only obliged to stage a revival of an old piece?'

Everything now depends on that. And the whole skill in handling the 'transference' is devoted to bringing it about. As you see, the requirements of analytic technique reach their maximum at this point. Here the gravest mistakes can be made or the greatest successes be registered. It would be folly to attempt to evade the difficulties by suppressing or neglecting the transference: whatever else had been done in the treatment, it would not deserve the name of an analysis. To send the patient away as soon as the inconveniences of his transference-neurosis make their appearance would be no more sensible, and would moreover be cowardly. It would be as though one had conjured up spirits and run away from them as soon as they appeared. Sometimes, it is true, nothing else is possible. There are cases in which one cannot master the unleashed transference and the analysis has to be broken off; but one must at least have struggled with the evil spirits to the best of one's strength. To yield to the demands of the transference, to fulfil the patient's wishes for affectionate and sensual satifaction, is not only justly forbidden by moral considerations but is also completely ineffective as a technical method for attaining the purpose of the analysis. A neurotic cannot be cured by being enabled to reproduce uncorrected an unconscious stereotype plate that is ready to hand in him. If one engages in compromises with him by offering him partial satisfactions in exchange for his further collaboration in the analysis, one must beware of falling into the ridiculous situation of the cleric who was supposed to convert a sick insurance agent. The sick man remained unconverted but the cleric took his leave insured. The only possible way out of the transference situation is to trace it back to the patient's past, as he really experienced it or as he pictured it through the wish-fulfilling activity of his imagination.

And this demands from the analyst much skill, patience, calm, and self-abnegation.

'And where do you suppose the neurotic experienced the prototype of his transference-love?'

In his childhood: as a rule in his relation with one of his parents. You will remember what importance we had to attribute to these earliest emotional ties. So here the circle closes.

'Have you finished at last? I am feeling just a little bewildered with all I have heard from you. Only tell me one thing more: how and where can one learn what is necessary for practising analysis?'

There are at the moment two Institutes at which instruction in psycho-analysis is given. The first has been founded in Berlin by Dr Max Eitingon, who is a member of the Society there. The second is maintained by the Vienna Psycho-Analytical Society at its own expense and at considerable sacrifice. The part played by the authorities is at present limited to the many difficulties which they put in the way of the young undertaking. A third training Institute is at this moment being opened in London by the Society there, under the direction of Dr Ernest Jones. At these Institutes the candidates themselves are taken into analysis, receive theoretical instruction by lectures on all the subjects that are important for them, and enjoy the supervision of older and more experienced analysts when they are allowed to make their first trials with comparatively slight cases. A period of some two years is calculated for this training. Even after this period, of course, the candidate is only a beginner and not yet a master. What is still needed must be acquired by practice and by an exchange of ideas in the psycho-analytical societies in which young and old members meet together. Preparation for analytic activity is by no means so easy and simple. The work is hard, the responsibility great. But anyone who has passed through such a course of instruction, who has been analysed himself, who has mastered what can be taught today of the psychology of the unconscious, who is at home in the science of sexual life, who has learnt the delicate technique of psycho-analysis, the art of interpretation, of fighting resistances, and of handling the transference – anyone who has accomplished all this *is no longer a layman in the field of psycho-analysis*. He is capable of undertaking the treatment of neurotic disorders, and will be able in time to achieve in that field whatever can be required from this form of therapy.

VI

'You have expended a great deal of effort on showing me what psycho-analysis is and what sort of knowledge is needed in order to practise it with some prospect of success. Very well. Listening to you can have done me no harm. But I do not know what influence on my judgement you expect your explanations to have. I see before me a case which has nothing unusual about it. The neuroses are a particular kind of illness and analysis is a particular method of treating them – a specialized branch of medicine. It is the rule in other cases as well for a doctor who has chosen a special branch of medicine not to be satisfied with the education that is confirmed by his diploma: particularly if he intends to set up in a fairly large town, such as can alone offer a livelihood to specialists. Anyone who wants to be a surgeon tries to work for a few years at a surgical clinic, and similarly with oculists, laryngologists, and so on – to say nothing of psychiatrists, who are perhaps never able to get away from a state institution or a sanatorium. And the same will happen in the case of psycho-analysts: anyone who decides in favour of this new specialized branch of medicine will, when his studies are completed, take on the two years' training you spoke of in a training institute, if it really requires so much time. He will realize afterwards, too, that it is to his advantage to keep up his contact with his colleagues in a psycho-analytical society, and everything will go along swimmingly. I cannot see where there is a place in this for the question of lay analysis.'

A doctor who does what you have promised on his behalf will be welcome to all of us. Four-fifths of those whom I recognize as my pupils are in any case doctors. But allow me to point out to you how the relations of doctors to analysis have really developed and how they will probably continue to develop. Doctors have no historical claim to the sole possession of analysis. On the contrary, until recently they have met it with everything possible that could damage it, from the shallowest ridicule to the gravest calumny. You will justly reply that that belongs to the past and need not affect the future. I agree, but I fear the future will be different from what you have foretold.

Permit me to give the word 'quack' the meaning it ought to have instead of the legal one. According to the law a quack is anyone who treats patients without possessing a state diploma to prove he is a doctor. I should prefer another definition: a quack is anyone who undertakes a treatment without possessing the knowledge and capacities necessary for it. Taking my stand on this definition, I venture to assert that – not only in European countries – doctors form a preponderating contingent of quacks in analysis. They very frequently practise analytic treatment without having learnt it and without understanding it.

It is no use your objecting that that is unconscientious and that you cannot believe doctors capable of it; that after all a doctor knows that a medical diploma is not a letter of marque* and that a patient is not an outlaw; and that one must always grant to a doctor that he is acting in good faith even if he may perhaps be in error.

The facts remain; we will hope that they can be accounted for as you think. I will try to explain to you how it becomes possible for a doctor to act in connexion with psycho-analysis in a manner which he would carefully avoid in every other field.

The first consideration is that in his medical school a doctor receives a training which is more or less the opposite of what he would need as a preparation for psycho-analysis. His attention has been directed to objectively ascertainable facts of anatomy, physics, and chemistry, on the correct

*[i.e. does not give him a privateer's licence.]

appreciation and suitable influencing of which the success of medical treatment depends. The problem of life is brought into his field of vision so far as it has hitherto been explained to us by the play of forces which can also be observed in inanimate nature. His interest is not aroused in the mental side of vital phenomena; medicine is not concerned with the study of the higher intellectual functions, which lies in the sphere of another faculty. Only psychiatry is supposed to deal with the disturbances of mental functions; but we know in what manner and with what aims it does so. It looks for the somatic determinants of mental disorders and treats them like other causes of illness.

Psychiatry is right to do so and medical education is clearly excellent. If it is described as one-sided, one must first discover the standpoint from which one is making that characteristic into a reproach. In itself every science is one-sided. It must be so, since it restricts itself to particular subjects, points of view, and methods. It is a piece of nonsense in which I would take no part to play off one science against another. After all, physics does not diminish the value of chemistry; it cannot take its place but on the other hand cannot be replaced by it. Psycho-analysis is certainly quite particularly one-sided, as being the science of the mental unconscious. We must not therefore dispute to the medical sciences their right to be one-sided.

We shall only find the standpoint we are in search of if we turn from scientific medicine to practical therapeutics. A sick person is a complicated organism. He may remind us that even the mental phenomena which are so hard to grasp should not be effaced from the picture of life. Neurotics, indeed, are an undesired complication, an embarrassment as much to therapeutics as to jurisprudence and to military service. But they exist and are a particular concern of medicine. Medical education, however, does nothing, literally nothing, towards their understanding and treatment. In view of the intimate connexion between the things that we distinguish as physical and mental, we may look forward to a day when paths of knowledge and, let us hope, of influence will be opened up, leading from organic biology and chemistry to the field of neurotic phenomena. That day still seems a distant one, and for the present these illnesses are inaccesible to us from the direction of medicine.

It would be tolerable if medical education merely failed to give doctors any orientation in the field of the neuroses. But it does more: it gives them a false and detrimental attitude. Doctors whose interest has not been aroused in the psychical factors of life are all too ready to form a low estimate of them and to ridicule them as unscientific. For that reason they are unable to take anything really seriously which has to do with them and do not recognize the obligations which derive from them. They therefore fall into the layman's lack of respect for psychological research and make their own task easy for themselves. – No doubt neurotics have to be treated, since they are sick people and come to the doctor; and one must always be ready to experiment with something new. But why burden oneself with a tedious preparation? We shall manage all right; who can tell if what they teach in the analytic institutes is any good? – The less such doctors understand about the matter, the more venturesome they become. Only a man who really knows is modest, for he knows how insufficient his knowledge is.

The comparison which you brought up to pacify me, between specialization in analysis and in other branches of medicine, is thus not applicable. For surgery, ophthalmology, and so on, the medical school itself offers an opportunity for further education. The analytic training institutes are few in number, young in years, and without authority. The medical schools have not recognized them and take no notice of them. The young doctor, who has had to take so much on trust from his teachers that he has had little

occasion for educating his judgement, will gladly seize an
occasion for playing the part of a critic for once in a field in
which there is as yet no recognized authority.

There are other things too that favour his appearing as
an analytic quack. If he tried to undertake eye-operations
without sufficient preparation, the failure of his cataract
extractions and iridectomies and the absence of patients
would soon bring his hazardous enterprise to an end. The
practice of analysis is comparatively safe for him. The
public is spoilt by the average successful outcome of eye-
operations and expects cure from the surgeon. But if a
'nerve-specialist' fails to restore his patients no one is surprised. People have not been spoilt by successes in the
therapy of the neuroses; the nerve-specialist has at least
'taken a lot of trouble with them'. Indeed, there is not much
that can be done; nature must help, or time. With women
there is first menstruation, then marriage, and later on the
menopause. Finally death is a real help. Moreover, what the
medical analyst has done with his neurotic patient is so
inconspicuous that no reproach can attach to it. He has
made use of no instruments or medicines; he has merely
conversed with him and tried to talk him into or out of
something. Surely that can do no harm, especially if he
avoids touching on distressing or agitating subjects. The
medical analyst, who has avoided any strict teaching, will,
no doubt, not have omitted an attempt to improve
analysis, to pull out its poison fangs and make it pleasant
for the patient. And it will be wise for him to stop there:
for if he really ventures to call up resistances and then does
not know how to meet them, he may in true earnest make
himself unpopular.

Honesty compels me to admit that the activity of an un-
trained analyst does less harm to his patients than that of an
unskilled surgeon. The possible damage is limited to the patient having been led into useless expenditure and having his
chances of recovery removed or diminished. Furthermore,

the reputation of analytic therapy has been lowered. All this is most undesirable, but it bears no comparison with the dangers that threaten from the knife of a surgical quack. In my judgement, severe or permanent aggravations of a pathological condition are not to be feared even with an unskilled use of analysis. The unwelcome reactions cease after a while. Compared with the traumas of life which have provoked the illness, a little mishandling by the doctor is of no account. It is simply that the unsuitable attempt at a cure has done the patient no good.

'I have listened to your account of the medical quack in analysis without interrupting you, though I formed an impression that you are dominated by a hostility against the medical profession to the historical explanation of which you yourself have pointed the way. But I will grant you one thing: if analyses are to be carried out, it should be by people who have been thoroughly trained for it. And do you not think that with time the doctors who turn to analysis will do everything to obtain that training?'

I fear not. So long as the attitude of the medical school to the analytic training institute remains unaltered, doctors will find the temptation to make things easier for themselves too great.

'But you seem to be consistently evading any direct pronouncement on the question of lay analysis. What I guess now is that, because it is impossible to keep a check on doctors who want to analyse, you are proposing, out of revenge, as it were, to punish them by depriving them of their monopoly in analysis and by throwing open this medical activity to laymen as well.'

I cannot say whether you have guessed my motives correctly. Perhaps I shall be able later on to put evidence before you of a less partial attitude. But I lay stress on the demand that *no one should practise analysis who has not acquired the right to do so by a particular training.* Whether such a person is a doctor or not seems to me immaterial.

'Then what definite proposals have you to make?'

I have not got so far as that yet; and I cannot tell whether I shall get there at all. I should like to discuss another question with you, and first of all to touch on one special point. It is said that the authorities, at the instigation of the medical profession, want to forbid the practice of analysis by laymen altogether. Such a prohibition would also affect the non-medical members of the Psycho-Analytical Society, who have enjoyed an excellent training and have perfected themselves greatly by practice. If the prohibition were enacted, we should find ourselves in a position in which a number of people are prevented from carrying out an activity which one can safely feel convinced they can perform very well, while the same activity is opened to other people for whom there is no question of a similar guarantee. That is not precisely the sort of result to which legislation should lead. However, this special problem is neither very important nor difficult to solve. Only a handful of people are concerned, who cannot be seriously damaged. They will probably emigrate to Germany where no legislation will prevent them from finding recognition for their proficiency. If it is desired to spare them this and to mitigate the law's severity, that can easily be done on the basis of some well-known precedents. Under the Austrian Monarchy it repeatedly happened that permission was given to notorious quacks, *ad personam* [personally], to carry out medical activities in certain fields, because people were convinced of their real ability. Those concerned were for the most part peasant healers, and their recommendation seems regularly to have been made by one of the Archduchesses who were once so numerous; but it ought to be possible for it also to be done in the case of town-dwellers and on the basis of a different and merely expert guarantee. Such a prohibition would have more important effects on the Vienna analytic training institute, which would thenceforward be unable to accept any candidates for training from non-medical circles. Thus once again in our country a line of intellectual activity would be suppressed which is allowed to develop freely elsewhere. I am the last person to claim any competence in judging laws and regulations. But this much I can see: that to lay emphasis on our quackery law does not lead in the direction of the approach to conditions in Germany which is so much aimed at today,* and that the application of that law to the case of psychoanalysis has something of an anachronism about it, since at the time of its enactment there was as yet no such thing as analysis and the peculiar nature of neurotic illnesses was not yet recognized.

I come now to a question the discussion of which seems to me more important. Is the practice of psycho-analysis a matter which should in general be subject to official interference, or would it be more expedient to leave it to follow its natural development? I shall certainly not come to any decision on this point here and now, but I shall take the liberty of putting the problem before you for your consideration. In our country from of old a positive *furor prohibendi* [passion for prohibitions] has been the rule, a tendency to keep people under tutelage, to interfere and to forbid, which, as we all know, has not borne particularly good fruit. In our new republican Austria, it seems things have not yet changed very much. I fancy you will have an important word to say in deciding the case of psycho-analysis which we are now considering; I do not know whether you have the wish or the influence with which to oppose these bureaucratic tendencies. At all events, I shall not spare you my unauthoritative thoughts on the subject. In my opinion a superabundance of regulations and prohibitions injures the authority of the law. It can be observed that where only a few prohibitions exist they are carefully observed, but where one is accompanied by prohibitions at every step, one feels definitely tempted to disregard them. Moreover,

*[This of course was in the days of the Weimar republic.]

it does not mean one is quite an anarchist if one is prepared
to realize that laws and regulations cannot from their origin
claim to possess the attribute of being sacred and untrans-
gressable, that they are often inadequtely framed and offend
our sense of justice, or will do so after a time, and that, in
view of the sluggishness of the authorities, there is often no
other means of correcting such inexpedient laws than by
boldly violating them. Furthermore, if one desires to maintain respect for laws and regulations it is advisable not to
enact any where a watch cannot easily be kept on whether
they are obeyed or transgressed. Much of what I have
quoted above on the practice of analysis by doctors could
be repeated here in regard to genuine analysis by laymen
which the law is seeking to suppress. The course of analysis
is most inconspicuous, it employs neither medicines nor
instruments and consists only in talking and an exchange
of information; it will not be easy to prove that a layman is
practising 'analysis' if he asserts that he is merely giving
encouragement and explanations and trying to establish a
healthy human influence on people who are in search of
mental assistance. It would surely not be possible to forbid
that merely because doctors sometimes do the same thing.
In English-speaking countries the practices of Christian
Science have become very widespread : a kind of dialectical
denial of the evils in life, based on an appeal to the doctrines
of the Christian religion. I do not hesitate to assert that
that procedure represents a regrettable aberration of the
human spirit; but who in America or England would dream
of forbidding it and making it punishable ? Are the authorities so certain of the right path to salvation that they venture to prevent each man from trying 'to be saved after his
own fashion' ?* And granted that many people if they are
left to themselves run into danger and come to grief, would
not the authorities do better carefully to mark the limits of

*[The saying 'In my State every man can be saved after his own
fashion' is attributed to Frederick the Great.]

the regions which are to be regarded as not to be trespassed upon, and for the rest, so far as possible, to allow human beings to be educated by experience and mutual influence? Psycho-analysis is something so new in the world, the mass of mankind is so little instructed about it, the attitude of official science to it is still so vacillating, that it seems to me over-hasty to intervene in its development with legislative regulations. Let us allow patients themselves to discover that it is damaging to them to look for mental assistance to people who have not learnt how to give it. If we explain this to them and warn them against it, we shall have spared ourselves the need to forbid it. On the main roads of Italy the pylons that carry high-tension cables bear the brief and impressive inscription: '*Chi tocca, muore* [He who touches will die].' This is perfectly calculated to regulate the behaviour of passers-by to any wires that may be hanging down. The corresponding German notices exhibit an unnecessary and offensive verbosity: '*Das Berühren der Lietungsdrähte ist, weil lebensgefährlich, strengstens verboten* [Touching the transmission cables is, since it is dangerous to life, most strictly prohibited].' Why the prohibition? Anyone who holds his life dear will make the prohibition for himself; and anyone who wants to kill himself in that way will not ask for permission.

'But there are instances that can be quoted as legal precedents against allowing lay analysis; I mean the prohibition against laymen practising hypnotism and the recently enacted prohibition against holding spiritualist séances or founding spiritualist societies.'

I cannot say that I am an admirer of these measures. The second one is a quite undisguised encroachment of police supervision to the detriment of intellectual freedom. I am beyond suspicion of having much belief in what are known as 'occult phenomena' or of feeling any desire that they should be recognized. But prohibitions like these will not stifle people's interest in that supposedly mysterious world.

They may on the contrary have done much harm and have closed the door to an impartial curiosity which might have arrived at a judgement that would have set us free from these harassing possibilities. But once again this only applies to Austria. In other countries 'para-psychical' researches are not met by any legal obstacles. The case of hypnotism is somewhat different from that of analysis. Hypnotism is the evoking of an abnormal mental state and is used by laymen today only for the purpose of public shows. If hypnotic therapy had maintained its very promising beginnings a position would have been arrived at similar to that of analysis. And incidentally the history of hypnotism provides a precedent for that of analysis in another direction. When I was a young lecturer in neuropathology, the doctors inveighed passionately against hypnotism, declared that it was a swindle, a deception of the Devil's, and a highly dangerous procedure. Today they have monopolized this same hypnotism and they make use of it unhesitatingly as a method of examination; for some nerve specialists it is still their chief therapeutic instrument.

But I have already told you that I have no intention of making proposals which are based on the decision as to whether legal control or letting things go is to be preferred in the matter of analysis. I know this is a question of principle on the reply to which the inclinations of persons in authority will probably have more influence than arguments. I have already set out what seems to me to speak in favour of a policy of *laissez faire*. If the other decision is taken – for a policy of active intervention – then it seems to me that in any case a lame and unjust measure of ruthlessly forbidding analysis by non-doctors will be an insufficient outcome. More will have to be considered in that case: the conditions will have to be laid down under which the practice of analysis shall be permitted to all those who seek to make use of it, an authority will have to be set up from whom one can learn what analysis is and what sort of

preparation is needed for it, and the possibilities for instruction in analysis will have to be encouraged. We must therefore either leave things alone or establish order and clarity;
we must not rush into a complicated situation with a single
isolated prohibition derived mechanically from a regulation
that has become inadequate.

VII

'YES, but the doctors! the doctors! I cannot induce you to go into the real subject of our conversations. You still keep on evading me. It is a question of whether we should not give doctors the exclusive right of practising analysis – for all I care, after they have fulfilled certain conditions. The majority of doctors are certainly not quacks in analysis as you have represented them. You say yourself that the great majority of your pupils and followers are doctors. It has come to my ears that they are far from sharing your point of view on the question of lay analysis. I may no doubt assume that your pupils agree with your demands for sufficient preparation and so on; and yet these pupils think it consistent to close the practice of analysis to laymen. Is that so? and if so, how do you explain it?'

I see you are well informed. Yes, it is so. Not all, it is true, but a good proportion of my medical colleagues do not agree with me over this, and are in favour of doctors having an exclusive right to the analytic treatment of neurotics. This will show you that differences of opinion are allowed even in our camp. The side I take is well-known, and the contradiction on the subject of lay analysis does not interfere with our good understanding. How can I explain the attitude of these pupils of mine to you? I do not know for certain; I think it must be the power of professional feeling. The course of their development has been different from mine, they still feel uncomfortable in their isolation from their colleagues, they would like to be accepted by the 'profession' as having plenary rights, and are prepared, in exchange for that tolerance, to make a sacrifice at a point whose vital importance is not obvious to them. Perhaps it may be otherwise; to impute motives of competition to them would be not only to accuse them of base sentiments but also to attribute a strange shortsightedness to them. They are always ready to introduce other doctors into analysis, and from a material point of view it must be a matter of indifference to them whether they have to share the available patients with medical colleagues or with lay-men. But something different probably plays a part. These pupils of mine may be influenced by certain factors which guarantee a doctor an undoubted advantage over a layman in analytic practice.

'Guarantee him an advantage? There we have it. So you are admitting the advantage at last? This should settle the question.'

The admission is not hard for me to make. It may show you that I am not so passionately prejudiced as you suppose. I have put off mentioning these things because their discussion will once again make theoretical considerations necessary.

'What are you thinking of now?'

First there is the question of diagnosis. When one takes into analysis a patient suffering from what are described as nervous disorders, one wishes beforehand to be certain — so far, of course, as certainty can be attained — that he is suited for this kind of treatment, that one can help him, that is to say, by this method. That, however, is only the case if he really has a neurosis.

'I should have thought that would be recognizable from the phenomena, the symptoms, of which he complains.'

This is where a fresh complication arises. It cannot always be recognized with complete certainty. The patient may exhibit the external picture of a neurosis, and yet it may be something else — the beginning of an incurable mental disease or the preliminary of a destructive process in the brain. The distinction — the differential diagnosis — is not always easy and cannot be made immediately in every phase. The responsibility for such a decision can of course only be undertaken by a doctor. As I have said, it is not always easy for him. The illness may have an innocent appearance for a considerable time, till in the end it after all displays its evil character. Indeed, it is one of the regular fears of neurotics that they may become insane. However, if a doctor has been mistaken for a time over a case of this sort or has been in uncertainty about it, no harm has been caused and nothing unnecessary has been done. Nor indeed would the analytic treatment of this case have done any harm, though it would have been exposed as an unnecessary waste. And moreover there would certainly be enough people who would blame the analysis for the unfortunate outcome. Unjustly, no doubt, but such occasions ought to be avoided.

'But that sounds hopeless. It strikes at the roots of everything you have told me about the nature and origin of a neurosis.'

Not at all. It merely confirms once again the fact that neurotics are a nuisance and an embarrassment for all concerned – including the analysts. But perhaps I shall clear up your confusion if I state my new information in more correct terms. It would probably be more correct to say of the cases we are now dealing with that they have really developed a neurosis, but that it is not psychogenic but somatogenic – that its causes are not mental but physical. Do you understand?

'Oh, yes, I understand. But I cannot bring it into harmony with the other side, the psychological one.'

That can be managed, though, if one bears in mind the complexities of living substance. In what did we find the essence of a neurosis? In the fact that the ego, the higher organization of the mental apparatus (elevated through the influence of the external world), is not able to fulfil its function of mediating between the id and reality, that in its feebleness it draws back from some instinctual portions of the id and, to make up for this, has to put up with the consequences of its renunciation in the form of restrictions, symptoms, and unsuccessful reaction-formations.

A feebleness of the ego of this sort is to be found in all of us in childhood; and that is why the experiences of the earliest years of childhood are of such great importance for later life. Under the extraordinary burden of this period of childhood – we have in a few years to cover the enormous developmental distance between stone-age primitive men and the participants in contemporary civilization, and, at the same time and in particular, we have to fend off the instinctual impulses of the early sexual period – under this burden, then, our ego takes refuge in repression and lays itself open to a childhood neurosis, the precipitate of which it carries with it into maturity as a disposition to a later nervous illness. Everything now depends on how the growing organism is treated by fate. If life becomes too hard, if the gulf between instinctual claims and the demands of reality becomes too great, the ego may fail in its efforts to reconcile the two, and the more readily, the more it is inhibited by the disposition carried over by it from infancy. The process of repression is then repeated, the instincts tear themselves away from the ego's domination, find their substitutive satisfactions along the paths of regression, and the poor ego has become helplessly neurotic.

Only let us hold fast to this: the nodal point and pivot of the whole situation is the relative strength of the ego organization. We shall then find it easy to complete our aetiological survey. As what may be called the normal causes of neurotic illness we already know the feebleness of the childhood ego, the task of dealing with the early sexual impulses, and the effects of the more or less chance experiences of childhood. Is it not possible, however, that yet other factors play a part, derived from the time before the beginning of the child's life? For instance, an innate strength and unruliness of the instinctual life in the id, which from the outset sets the ego tasks too hard for it? Or a special developmental feebleness of the ego due to unknown reasons? Such factors must of course acquire an aetiological importance, in some cases a transcendent one. We have invariably to reckon with the instinctual strength of the id; if it has developed to excess, the prospects of our therapy are poor. We still know too little of the causes of a developmental inhibition of the ego. These then would be the cases of neurosis with an essentially constitutional basis. Without some such constitutional, congenital favouring factors a neurosis can, no doubt, scarcely come about.

But if the relative feebleness of the ego is the decisive factor for the genesis of a neurosis, it must also be possible for a later physical illness to produce a neurosis, provided that it can bring about an enfeeblement of the ego. And that, once again, is very frequently found. A physical disorder of this kind can affect the instinctual life in the id and increase the strength of the instincts beyond the limit up to which the ego is capable of coping with them. The normal model of such processes is perhaps the alteration in women caused by the disturbances of menstruation and the menopause. Or again, a general somatic illness, indeed an organic disease of the nervous central organ, may attack the nutritional conditions of the mental apparatus and compel it to reduce its functioning and to bring to a halt its more delicate workings, one of which is the maintenance of the ego organization. In all these cases approximately the same picture of neurosis emerges; neurosis always has the same psychological mechanism, but, as we see, a most varied and often very complex aetiology.

'You please me better now. You have begun talking like a doctor at last. And now I expect you to admit that such a complicated medical affair as a neurosis can only be handled by a doctor.'

I fear you are overshooting the mark. What we have been discussing was a piece of pathology, what we are concerned with in analysis is a therapeutic procedure. I allow – no, I insist – that in every case which is under consideration for analysis the diagnosis shall be established first by a doctor. By far the greater number of neuroses which occupy us are fortunately of a psychogenic nature and give no grounds for pathological suspicions. Once the doctor has established this, he can confidently hand over the treatment to a lay analyst. In our analytical societies matters have always been arranged in that way. Thanks to the intimate contact between medical and non-medical members, mistakes such as might be feared have been as good as completely avoided. There is a further contingency, again, in which the analyst has to ask the doctor's help. In the course of an analytic treatment, symptoms – most often physical symptoms – may appear about which one is doubtful whether they should be regarded as belonging to the neurosis or whether they should be related to an independent organic illness that has intervened. The decision on this point must once again be left to a doctor.

'So that even during the course of analysis a lay analyst cannot do without a doctor. A fresh argument against their fitness.'

No. No argument against lay analysts can be manufactured out of this possibility, for in such circumstances a medical analyst would not act differently.

'I do not understand that.'

There is a technical rule that an analyst, if dubious symptoms like this emerge during the treatment, shall not submit them to his own judgement but shall get them reported upon by a doctor who is not connected with analysis – a consultant physician, perhaps – even if the analyst himself is a doctor and still well-versed in his medical knowledge.

'And why should a rule be made that seems to me so uncalled-for ?'

It is not uncalled-for; in fact there are several reasons for it. In the first place it is not a good plan for a combination of organic and psychical treatment to be carried out by one and the same person. Secondly the relation in the transference may make it inadvisable for the analyst to examine the patient physically. And thirdly the analyst has every reason for doubting whether he is unprejudiced, since his interests are directed so intensely to the psychical factors.

'I now understand your attitude to lay analysis quite clearly. You are determined that there must be lay analysts. And since you cannot dispute their inadequacy for their task, you are scraping together everything you can to excuse them and make their existence easier. But I cannot in the least see why there should be lay analysts, who, after all, can only be therapists of the second class. I am ready, so far as I am concerned, to make an exception in the case of the few laymen who have already been trained as analysts; but no fresh ones should be created and the training institutes should be put under an obligation to take no more laymen into training.'

I am at one with you, if it can be shown that all the interests involved will be served by this restriction. You will agree that these interests are of three sorts: that of the patients, that of the doctors, and – last but not least – that of science, which indeed comprises the interests of all future patients. Shall we examine these three points together?

For the patient, then, it is a matter of indifference whether the analyst is a doctor or not, provided only that the danger of his condition being misunderstood is excluded by the necessary medical reports before the treatment begins and on some possible occasions during the course of it. For him it is incomparably more important that the analyst should possess personal qualities that make him trustworthy, and that he should have acquired the knowledge and understanding as well as the experience which alone can make it possible for him to fulfill his task. It might be thought that it would damage an analyst's authority if the patient knows that he is not a doctor and cannot in some situations do without a doctor's support. We have, of course, never omitted to inform patients of their analyst's qualification, and we have been able to convince ourselves that professional prejudices find no echo in them and that they are ready to accept a cure from whatever direction it is offered them – which, incidentally, the medical profession discovered long ago to its deep mortification. Nor are the lay analysts who practise analysis today any chance collection of riff-raff, but people of academic education, doctors of philosophy, educationists, together with a few women of great experience in life and outstanding personality. The analysis, to which all the candidates in an analytic training institute have to submit, is at the same time the best means of forming an opinion of their personal aptitude for carrying out their exacting occupation.

Now as to the interest of the doctors. I cannot think that it would gain by the incorporation of psycho-analysis into medicine. The medical curriculum already lasts for five years and the final examinations extend well into a sixth year. Every few years fresh demands are made on the student, without the fulfilment of which his equipment for the future would have to be declared insufficient. Access to the medical profession is very difficult and its practice neither satisfying nor very remunerative. If one supports what is certainly a fully justified demand that doctors should also be familiar with the mental side of illness, and if on that account one extends medical education to include some preparation for analysis, that implies a further increase in the curriculum and a corresponding prolongation of the period of study. I do not know whether the doctors will be pleased by this consequence of their claim upon analysis. But it can scarcely be escaped. And this at a period in which the conditions of material existence have so greatly deteriorated for the classes from which doctors are recruited, a period in which the younger generation sees itself compelled to make itself self-supporting as early in life as possible.

But perhaps you will choose not to burden medical studies with the preparation for analytic practice but think it more expedient for future analysts to take up their necessary training only after the end of their medical studies. You may say the loss of time involved in this is of no practical account, since after all a young man of less than thirty will never enjoy his patients' confidence, which is a *sine qua non* of giving mental assistance. It might no doubt be said in reply that a newly-fledged physician for physical illnesses cannot count upon being treated by his patients with very great respect either, and that a young analyst might very well fill in his time by working in a psycho-analytic outpatient clinic under the supervision of experienced practitioners.

But what seems to me more important is that with this proposal of yours you are giving support to a waste of energy for which, in these difficult times, I can really find no economic justification. Analytic training, it is true, cuts across the field of medical education, but neither includes the other. If – which may sound fantastic today – one had to found a college of psycho-analysis, much would have to be taught in it which is also taught by the medical faculty: alongside of depth-psychology, which would always remain the principal subject, there would be an introduction to biology, as much as possible of the science of sexual life, and familiarity with the symptomatology of psychiatry. On the other hand, analytic instruction would include branches of knowledge which are remote from medicine and which the doctor does not come across in his practice: the history of civilization, mythology, the psychology of religion and the science of literature. Unless he is well at home in these subjects, an analyst can make nothing of a large amount of his material. By way of compensation, the great mass of what is taught in medical schools is of no use to him for his purposes. A knowledge of the anatomy of the tarsal bones, of the constitution of the carbohydrates, of the course of the cranial nerves, a grasp of all that medicine has brought to light on bacilli as exciting causes of disease and the means of combating them, on serum reactions and on neoplasms – all this knowledge, which is undoubtedly of the highest value in itself, is nevertheless of no consequence to him; it does not concern him; it neither helps him directly to understand a neurosis and to cure it nor does it contribute to a sharpening of those intellectual capacities on which his occupation makes the greatest demands. It cannot be objected that the case is much the same when a doctor takes up some other special branch of medicine – dentistry, for instance: in that case, too, he may not need some of what he has to pass examinations in, and he will have to learn much in addition, for which his schooling has not prepared him. But the two cases cannot be put on a par. In dentistry the great principles of pathology – the theories of inflammation, suppuration, necrosis, and of the metabolism of the bodily organs – still retain their importance. But the experience of an analyst lies in another world, with other phenomena and other laws. However much philosophy may ignore the gulf between the physical and the mental, it still exists for our immediate experience and still more for our practical endeavours.

It is unjust and inexpedient to try to compel a person who wants to set someone else free from the torment of a phobia or an obsession to take the roundabout road of the medical curriculum. Nor will such an endeavour have any success, unless it results in suppressing analysis entirely. Imagine a landscape in which two paths lead to a hilltop with a view – one short and straight, the other long, winding, and circuitous. You try to stop up the short path by a prohibitory notice, perhaps because it passes by some flower-beds that you want to protect. The only chance you have of your prohibition being respected is if the short path is steep and difficult while the longer one leads gently up. If, however, that is not so, and the roundabout path is on the contrary the harder, you may imagine the value of your prohibition and the fate of your flower-beds! I fear you will succeed in compelling the laymen to study medicine just as little as I shall be able to induce doctors to learn analysis. For you know human nature as well as I do.

'If you are right, that analytic treatment cannot be carried out without special training, but that the medical curriculum cannot bear the further burden of a preparation for it, and that medical knowledge is to a great extent unnecessary for an analyst, how shall we achieve the ideal physician who shall be equal to all the tasks of his calling?'

I cannot foresee the way out of these difficulties, nor is it my business to point it out. I see only two things: first that analysis is an embarrassment to you and that the best thing would be for it not to exist – though neurotics, no doubt, are an embarrassment too; and secondly, that the interests of everyone concerned would for the time being be met if the doctors could make up their minds to tolerate a class of therapists which would relieve them of the tedium of treating the enormously common psychogenic neuroses while remaining in constant touch with them to the benefit of the patients.

'Is that your last word on the subject? or have you something more to say?'

Yes indeed. I wanted to bring up a third interest – the interest of science. What I have to say about that will concern you little; but, by comparison, it is of all the more importance to me.

For we do not consider it at all desirable for psycho-analysis to be swallowed up by medicine and to find its last resting-place in a text-book of psychiatry under the heading 'Methods of Treatment', alongside of procedures such as hypnotic suggestion, autosuggestion, and persuasion, which, born from our ignorance, have to thank the laziness and cowardice of mankind for their short-lived effects. It deserves a better fate and it may be hoped, will meet with

one. As a 'depth-psychology', a theory of the mental unconscious, it can become indispensible to all the sciences which
are concerned with the evolution of human civilization and
its major institutions such as art, religion, and the social
order. It has already, in my opinion, afforded these sciences
considerable help in solving their problems. But these are
only small contributions compared with what might be
achieved if historians of civilization, psychologists of religion, philologists, and so on would agree themselves to
handle the new instrument of research which is at their
service. The use of analysis for the treatment of the neuroses
is only one of its applications; the future will perhaps show
that it is not the most important one. In any case it would
be wrong to sacrifice all the other applications to this
single one, just because it touches on the circle of medical
interests.

For here a further prospect stretches ahead, which cannot
be encroached upon with impunity. If the representatives
of the various mental sciences are to study psycho-analysis
so as to be able to apply its methods and angles of approach
to their own material, it will not be enough for them to stop
short at the findings which are laid down in analytic literature. They must learn to understand analysis in the only
way that is possible – by themselves undergoing an analysis.
The neurotics who need analysis would thus be joined by a
second class of persons, who accept analysis from intellectual motives, but who will no doubt also welcome the
increase in their capacities which they will incidentally
achieve. To carry out these analyses a number of analysts
will be needed, for whom any medical knowledge will have
particularly little importance. But these 'teaching analysts'
– let us call them – will require to have had a particularly
careful education. If this is not to be stunted, they must be
given an opportunity of collecting experience from instructive and informative cases; and since healthy people who
also lack the motive of curiosity do not present themselves

for analysis, it is once more only upon neurotics that it will be possible for the teaching analysts – under careful supervision – to be educated for their subsequent non-medical activity. All this, however, requires a certain amount of freedom of movement, and is not compatible with petty restrictions.

Perhaps you do not believe in these purely theoretical interests of psycho-analysis or cannot allow them to affect the practical question of lay analysis. Then let me advise you that psycho-analysis has yet another sphere of application, which is outside the scope of the quackery law and to which the doctors will scarcely lay claim. Its application, I mean, to the bringing-up of children. If a child begins to show signs of an undesirable development, if it grows moody, refractory, and inattentive, the paediatrician and even the school doctor can do nothing for it, even if the child produces clear neurotic symptoms, such as nervousness, loss of appetite, vomiting, or insomnia. A treatment that combines analytic influence with educational measures, carried out by people who are not ashamed to concern themselves with the affairs in a child's world, and who understand how to find their way into a child's mental life, can bring about two things at once: the removal of the neurotic symptoms and the reversal of the change in character which had begun. Our recognition of the importance of these inconspicuous neuroses of children as laying down the disposition for serious illnesses in later life points to these child analyses as an excellent method of prophylaxis. Analysis undeniably still has its enemies. I do not know whether they have means at their command for stopping the activities of these educational analysts or analytic educationalists. I do not think it very likely; but one can never feel too secure.

Moreover, to return to our question of the analytic treatment of adult neurotics, even there we have not yet exhausted every line of approach. Our civilization imposes an almost intolerable pressure on us and it calls for a corrective. Is it too fantastic to expect that psycho-analysis in spite of its difficulties may be destined to the task of preparing mankind for such a corrective? Perhaps once more an American may hit on the idea of spending a little money to get the 'social workers' of his country trained analytically and to turn them into a band of helpers for combating the neuroses of civilization.

'Aha! a new kind of Salvation Army!'

Why not? Our imagination always follows patterns. The stream of eager learners who will then flow to Europe will be obliged to pass Vienna by, for here the development of analysis may have succumbed to a premature trauma of prohibition. You smile? I am not saying this as a bribe for your support. Not in the least. I know you do not believe me; nor can I guarantee that it will happen. But one thing I do know. It is by no means so important *what* decision you give on the question of lay analysis. It may have a local effect. But the things that really matter – the possibilities in psycho-analysis for *internal* development – can never be affected by regulations and prohibitions.

EXPOSITORY WORKS BY FREUD

1904. 'Freud's Psycho-Analytic Procedure'
1905. 'On Psychotherapy'
1906. 'My Views on the Part Played by Sexuality in the Aetiology of the Neuroses'
1909. *Five Lectures on Psycho-Analysis*
1911. 'On Psycho-Analysis' (Australasian Medical Congress)
1913. 'The Claims of Psycho-Analysis to Scientific Interest'
1914. 'On the History of the Psycho-Analytic Movement'
1915-17. *Introductory Lectures on Psycho-Analysis*
1922. Two Encyclopaedia Articles (Marcuse's *Handwörterbuch*)
1924. 'A Short Account of Psycho-Analysis' (*These Eventful Years*)
1925. *An Autobiographical Study* and Postscript (1935)
1926. *The Question of Lay Analysis*
  'Psycho-Analysis' (*Encyclopaedia Britannica*)
1932. *New Introductory Lectures on Psycho-Analysis*
1938. *An Outline of Psycho-Analysis*
  'Some Elementary Lessons in Psycho-Analysis'

BIBLIOGRAPHY

BELL, J. SANFORD (1902) 'A Preliminary Study of the Emotion of Love between the Sexes', *American Journal of Psychology*, XIII, 325.

BLEULER, E. (1908) 'Sexuelle Abnormitäten der Kinder', *Jahrbuch der Schweizerischen Gesellschaft für Schulgesundheitspflege*, IX, 623.

FERENCZI, S. (1909) 'Introjection and Transference', *First Contributions to Psycho-Analysis*, London, Hogarth Press, 1952, Chap. II.

FREUD, M. (1957) *Glory Reflected*, London, Angus and Robertson.

FREUD, S. (1891) *On Aphasia*, London, Imago Publishing Co., 1953. (1893) with BREUER, J. 'On the Psychical Mechanism of Hysterical Phenomena: Preliminary Communication', *Studies on Hysteria*.

(1895) with BREUER, J., *Studies on Hysteria*, London, Hogarth Press, 1956.

(1900) *The Interpretation of Dreams*, London, Allen and Unwin, 1955.

(1901) *The Psychopathology of Everyday Life*, Standard Edition, Vol. VI.

(1905) *Jokes and their Relation to the Unconscious*, London, Routledge and Kegan Paul, 1960.

(1905) *Three Essays on the Theory of Sexuality*, London, Hogarth Press, 1962.

(1909) 'Analysis of a Phobia in a Five-Year-Old Boy', in Standard Edition, Vol. X.

(1910) 'Contributions to the Psychology of Love, I', in Standard Edition, Vol. XI.

(1911) 'Psycho-Analytic Notes on a Case of Paranoia [Dr Schreber]', in Standard Edition, Vol. XII.

(1912–13) *Totem and Taboo*, London, Routledge and Kegan Paul, 1950.

(1914) 'On the History of the Psycho-Analytic Movement', in Standard Edition, Vol. XIV.

(1916–17) *Introductory Lectures on Psycho-Analysis*, London, Allen and Unwin, 1929.

(1918) 'From the History of an Infantile Neurosis ["The Wolf Man"]', in Standard Edition, Vol. XVII.

(1920) *Beyond the Pleasure Principle*, London, Hogarth Press, 1950.

(1921) *Group Psychology and the Analysis of the Ego*, London, Hogarth Press, 1959.

(1923) *The Ego and the Id*, London, Hogarth Press, 1962.

(1925) 'Josef Breuer (Obituary)', in Standard Edition, Vol. XIX.

(1926) *Inhibitions, Symptoms and Anxiety*, London, Hogarth Press, 1961.

(1927) *The Future of an Illusion*, London, Hogarth Press,

(1930) *Civilization and its Discontents*, London, Hogarth Press.

(1939) *Moses and Monotheism*, London, Hogarth Press, 1939.

(1949) *An Outline of Psycho-Analysis*, London, Hogarth Press.

(1954) *The Origins of Psycho-Analysis* (includes 'A Project for a Scientific Psychology', 1895), London, Hogarth Press.

(1961) *Letters (1873–1939)* edited by Ernst Freud, London, Hogarth Press.

JONES, ERNEST (1953-7) *Sigmund Freud, Life and Work* (3 vols.) London, Hogarth Press.

JUNG, C. G. (1909) (ed.) *Studies in Word-Association*, London, Heinemann, 1918.

(1910) 'Experiences Concerning the Psychic Life of the Child', in *Collected Papers on Analytic Psychology*, London, Baillière, Tindall, and Cox, 1916.

INDEX